CW01642603

The book, *A* ... *and Beliefs,* discusses th... d Chinese traditional p...

It is a book on pastoral care and discipleship as well as an instruction manual all rolled into one. It is a guidebook that helps us to make sense of why certain practices are acceptable while others are not. And the best part of it all is that this book provides biblical reasons for our decisions.

...This book is written for Christians seeking to live out their faith more fully. In no way does it advocate intolerance; neither is it offensive to those who belong to other faiths. This is particularly important at a time when a high premium is placed on religious harmony and tolerance.

— Rev Philip Lim Kian Leong
***Methodist Message,* August 2004**

From time to time I come across people with inquisitive questions, personal as well as theological, as to how best to handle certain traditions or cultural situation as Christians. Having read this book, *A Biblical Approach to Chinese Traditions and Beliefs,* and hearing feedback from other church members, the common view is that it provides helpful insights and suggestions, and offers a practical approach to applying Christian principles to Chinese traditions and beliefs in an easy-to-understand style. This book is a useful reference to have on any bookshelf.

— Rev John Loong
Holy Trinity Church

A BIBLICAL APPROACH TO

CHINESE TRADITIONS AND BELIEFS

DANIEL TONG

GENESIS

Published by Genesis Books
An imprint of ARMOUR Publishing Pte Ltd
Kent Ridge Post Office
P. O. Box 1193
Singapore 911107
Email: mail@armourpublishing.com
Website: www.armourpublishing.com

First reprint 2003
Second reprint 2003
Third reprint 2004
Fourth reprint 2004
Fifth reprint 2005

Printed in Singapore

ISBN 981-4045-92-6

Dedication

To the

Reverend Canon Frank Lomax,

my pastor, my friend,

and the late

Madam Siau Bee Ho,

my mother, my confidant

Contents

Foreword

The Preacher says, "Of making many books there is no end; and much study is a weariness of the flesh" (Ecclesiates 12:12, *King James Version*). Yet we are grateful that Daniel Tong has stretched the advice a bit further. He has painstakingly produced a book which will, no doubt, be of much help to many Chinese Christians who desire to share the Gospel with their loved ones and friends, but know full well the immense complexities and cultural and religious minefields in the process. Daniel, for the sake of the Gospel, and some of the anguish that Paul shared in Romans 9:1ff, has collated issues of faith and culture in his pastoral ministry and study, and courageously shared them in this book.

Undoubtedly, the author is more than aware that some of his observations, interpretations and conclusions might not be acceptable to all and sundry. That is not the point. Daniel is, first of all, concerned that whatever the case may be, we must not shy away from difficult issues. We must, however, not hold positions and views without taking seriously and objectively both biblical and cultural studies as well as recognising the underlying influence of emotion and traditions in the faith circles that we grow up or move in.

Above all, Daniel wants to share through this book — both as a biblical Christian and a Chinese — his passion for communicating and holding on to the full Gospel message. *A Biblical Approach to Chinese Traditions and Beliefs* does not provide easy or simplistic answers to questions or tensions of faith and culture, but it is definitely a responsible and laudable way forward. It is much needed in the midst of the re-emergence of ancient and historical cultures and religions as well as potential religious sensitivities and tensions in this great land of Asia.

Rt Revd Dr John Chew
Bishop, Diocese of Singapore

Preface

This book, written for Christians, seeks to provide some guidelines on the cultural practices that we may engage in and those that we may not. More importantly, it seeks to provide sound biblical reasons for the decisions taken either way. This is done in the hope that more of us may be freed to enjoy the aspects of our Chinese culture and heritage that are free from religious entanglement. It is also done that Christians may, at the same time, learn to make a stand for our Lord Jesus Christ in areas that contravene the teaching of the Word of God as recorded in the Bible. Between cultural heritage and God, Christians must choose God first and foremost, always.

Our Chinese culture and heritage is rich, yet it is hard for some Christians to fully embrace and enjoy it. What irony, and this is because much of our Chinese culture and heritage is so inextricably intertwined with religious philosophies and beliefs that Christians should not embrace. The struggle for Christians, therefore, lies in how we are to maintain an active appreciation of our cultural heritage without compromising our faith. Hence, we struggle with questions like how we are to show filial piety at funerals or celebrate the various Chinese festivals, without going against the teachings of and grieving our God by engaging in unscriptural rites and rituals. Faced with such issues, what hurts many Christians the most is the rebuke of loved ones who cannot understand our spiritual commitment.

There are no easy answers to these questions, primarily, I surmise, because much revolves around emotional human and family ties. Here, I would like to request the understanding of any non-Christian who may pick up and read this book. Please understand that, written for Christians, this book uses words and concepts drawn from the Bible that may not be accepted by those who are not Christians. The purpose, however, is not to be offensive, nor is it to teach intolerance towards those who hold to other religious beliefs. The goal is simply to help Christians live their faith to the fullest, while maintaining the fact that we come from an ethnic group with a long and rich heritage.

This book is drawn primarily from a course I conduct on understanding Chinese traditions and beliefs, and incorporates a major update of my earlier work, *Ancestral Veneration: A Handbook for Christians*. In it we will discuss the major festivals celebrated, the practice of ancestral worship and traditional Chinese medical care. Along with this, this book seeks to give a brief description of the main tenets of the religious philosophies that undergird these traditions. As you read this book, please do so with an open mind and a prayerful heart, and a desire to grow in faith. Search the Word of God and test all that is written in this book, and seek to discern the will of God.

My thanks to the many pastors who granted me the privilege of teaching the above-mentioned course in their churches. These opportunities have helped me in my reflection on the issues raised and discussed in this book, and I have learnt much from interacting with those who have attended the classes. My thanks too to Miss Mabel Lee for the time and effort put into transcribing my lectures. Most importantly, our Lord God is to be thanked for His daily guidance and blessing, and the awesome privilege of allowing me to be of some small service to Him.

Daniel Tong

Laying The Foundation

Chapter 1
A Centuries-old Debate

A Historical Problem

Chinese religious beliefs are not new, and certainly not unique to Singapore, the surrounding Asian region and many other parts of the world where Chinese communities exist, and they do present for Christian believers certain difficulties. Questions have arisen, for example, of whether or not one may bow before the deceased with joss sticks in hand as a mark of filial piety and respect, or participate in traditional funeral rites. Issues such as these have been debated for centuries and we would be badly mistaken to think of them as a new problem. In fact, ever since missionary work started in Asia, the acceptability of religious beliefs and cultural practices has been a constant subject of debate.

In many ways, the early Western pioneers who came to the East had the attitude that they were more civilized than the people of the East. This attitude of superiority stemmed, in part, from the fact that the merchants and traders from the West came with big ships, canons, guns and more advanced science and technology. Many who arrived in China, therefore, did not see any need to learn from the Chinese, holding instead to the idea that they had greater knowledge to share and impart. Unfortunately, some of the early churchmen who served as chaplains to the Westerners and as missionaries held to the same mindset. Hence, they too sought, consciously or unconsciously, not just to convert the Chinese to the Faith, but also to the Western way of life.

James Hudson Taylor (1832-1905)

James Hudson Taylor, a nineteenth-century Protestant missioner, however, advocated the need to appreciate and identify with the culture of the people that one is trying to reach out to. To be effective in reaching out to the Chinese, Taylor believed that he first had to learn to understand them and appreciate their ways. This perspective was drawn from the teaching of the Apostle Paul, who wrote, "For though I am free from all men, I have made myself a slave to all, that I might win the more..." (1 Corinthians 9:19ff). Taylor, therefore, dressed like the Chinese, learned their language and culture, and began to preach in the Chinese tongue. This requirement was applied to all who subsequently joined in his work and mission.

Matteo Ricci (1552-1610) and the Jesuits

Centuries before Taylor came along, however, Matteo Ricci, a Roman Catholic missioner to China and the region, was already advocating similar ideas. Ricci saw the worth of the Chinese culture and suggested that one should accept and adopt what was civilized and good in it. The Roman Catholic Society of Jesus (Jesuits) supported this idea and advocated the acceptability of ancestral tablets and the offering of joss sticks. In this, they were supported by the Roman Catholic declaration of 1659, the *Propaganda*, which advocated the adoption of local customs and dress, along with the study of local literature and beliefs. In the early days of Jesuit mission work in China, the Chinese found it easier to accept the Jesuits and their message, as they did not have to give up, among other things, the practice of ancestral worship.

In a similar vein, if I were to approach a non-Christian today and say, "There is no problem to your being a Christian and continuing with your ancestral worship," I would be making it easier for him to turn to Christ. If I were to say, however, "If you want to turn to Christ, you need to get rid of your ancestral tablets and idols," that same person would probably struggle a lot more with becoming a Christian.

The attitude and approach of the Jesuits upset other Roman Catholic missions, like the Dominicans and the Franciscans, which did not advocate any accommodation to the Chinese culture and beliefs. It did not take long before there arose a lobby to the Pope and the Roman Catholics back home in Rome to censure the Jesuits, on the grounds that they were advocating wrong teachings. Church history records this as *The Rites Controversy,* during which numerous arguments concerning the "cultural" rites, rituals and practices that a believer could or could not engage in were raised. Over the centuries, a number of decrees were passed for and against assimilating Chinese practices into the Church, the swing of the pendulum being dependent on whether it was the proponents or opponents writing in to the Church authorities at the time with their petitions and arguments.[1] Begun in 1633, the Controversy did not see closure till 1939.

In fact, this was not just an issue for believers in China. In Korea, the earliest believers had come to faith as a result of reading Christian literature written by Matteo Ricci. These believers followed the teaching of Ricci and adopted a more accepting and accommodating attitude towards local beliefs and practices. When this perspective was denounced, these believers decided to obey the Pope. As a result, they faced tremendous persecution. One such persecution took place in 1791, where over 400 scholars who had embraced Christianity were put to death because they turned away from all that was associated with ancestral worship. In 1801, more than 300 believers were executed for the same reason.

General Comments: Today, believers continue to wonder about the appropriateness of certain traditions and beliefs in the light of their new-found faith. Differing opinions exist even among Asians, depending on their being either English- or Chinese-educated, and on their awareness of and receptiveness to the ideas of spiritual warfare. For example, an English-educated minister might view the practice of *qigong* as having a demonic root and decide to have nothing whatsoever to do with it. A Chinese-educated minister, on the other hand, may well have no problems in organizing *qigong* classes for the elderly in the church (a situation that did occur), viewing it to be simply a traditional Chinese form of calisthenics. The debate has raged for centuries and we should make no presumption that we will end it with this book. The good thing is that whereas this debate has been largely carried out among Western commentators in the past, more and more Asian pastors and theologians are entering into it now to partner with their Western colleagues for a better understanding of the whole issue.

Attempted Solutions

Over the centuries, there have been many attempts to resolve the issues discussed in this book. One solution is the absolute rejection of anything and everything even remotely associated with a questionable belief or practice. For example, I know of people who have searched through their photo albums to remove and destroy all holiday pictures of themselves or their family taken against a backdrop of temples and religious figurines, etc. Another solution is to focus on the apparent good of traditional practices in the name of culture, while overlooking the deep-seated religious and superstitious beliefs associated with these so-called cultural practices. For example, one could well find in certain parts of the third world, oranges and *ang pows* (red packets) placed on the church altar during *Chun Jie* (Chinese New Year), or *qigong* classes/sessions organised by the church.

The Roman Catholic Concept of Accommodation

The Roman Catholics, right up to today, have been fairly accommodating and open to the adoption of various practices deemed to be cultural. I know, for example, of at least one Roman Catholic church that would, during *Chun Jie*, purchase mandarin oranges, bless them in a service and then give them to members to wish them a blessed *Chun Jie*. Part of the reason for this openness might well stem from the declaration of the First Vatican Council (1890) that, "to hold and teach that God, the beginning and the end of all things, may be certainly known by the natural lights of human reason by means of created things…known by everyone with facility, with firm assurance, and with no admixture of error". There is truth to this statement, but one is not to interpret it to mean that a person may find God in and through the practices and beliefs of other religions.

Roman 1:20 teaches us that the invisible attributes of God may be perceived in the very creation around us. Open your eyes, perceive the beauty, order and complexity of this world, and you must acknowledge that all creation did not come about by accident (be it the "big bang" theory or evolution), but by the careful ordering and making of God. The problem with humanity is that though we perceive that there must be some divine being behind the wonder of nature, instead of turning to look for the Creator, we turn and bow down to created things (Romans 1:21,23,25). The tendency to focus on the creature rather than the Creator is a problem with us to this very day, as people generally desire to look to something tangible that they can see and feel. Believers must, therefore, be very careful and selective in their accommodation of Chinese cultural practices.

Protestant Pride and Prejudice

Many Protestants have opted for the view that the bulk of traditional Chinese practices and beliefs is rooted in pagan beliefs, thereby advocating a total rejection of them. Sadly, this attitude is not the result of a serious study of Chinese religious and cultural contexts or the Word of God. Instead, it may be said that one of the main reasons for this rejection is prejudice. Protestant missioners came to Asia after fighting and debating over the removal of statues and icons within the Western church because too much attention and emphasis had been placed on them. Imagine their horror upon arrival to find statues and icons all around them. It was, therefore, natural for the missioners to automatically consider the Chinese statutes and icons as bad.

Protestants also tend to be wary of and reject much of the practices and culture of the Chinese because of the power encounters faced by pastors and missionaries while ministering to Chinese men and women steeped in cultural practices. Real-life experiences of people being spiritually oppressed and even possessed because they have engaged in Chinese martial arts or rites and rituals, or have been adopted by some deity, etc. are abundant. In many cases, the person in bondage is not set free until he renounces and makes a clear break from these practices. Such experiences are not easily disregarded and do lead one to wonder if there is something fundamentally wrong with some aspects of our Chinese traditions and beliefs.

Much of Chinese culture is deeply rooted in religious beliefs and superstitious practices, and one often finds it hard to differentiate between what is acceptable and what is not. To avoid confusion and misunderstanding (and probably questions and problems), the easiest thing to do is simply to get rid of everything. This, however, is not the best solution as in doing so, we throw the baby out with the bathwater. There is much in Chinese culture and tradition to be appreciated, for example, the development of Chinese civilization, our rich history and the emphasis on filial piety, etc. We simply need to learn to sift through and divorce from the cultural that which is religious and superstitious. In this way, we may no longer be accused of being "bananas", yellow on the outside and white on the inside — Chinese by birth and the pigmentation of our skin, but Western at heart and in thought.

Sifting Through the Maze

As Chinese, we should seek to understand, appreciate and maintain certain aspects of our traditional culture. To reject and dispose out of hand everything Chinese would impoverish us and simply reinforce the view that Christianity is the religion of the white man, a Western import that is to be rejected. As Christians, we know that this is not the case. Christianity is neither geographically (East or West) nor ethnically bound (Westerners or Asians). Christianity speaks of a living relationship with the Creator of the universe that is for everyone, the expression of which is largely dependent on our identity in Christ and choice. It is important, therefore, for us to work out and retain those aspects of our culture that are good and acceptable, and discard without regret any aspect that does not glorify or runs contrary to the Word of God. To help us do this, we must seek to understand more about our Chinese culture and its traditions and practices.

One way of going about this is to examine the social, cultural and religious backgrounds of the various traditions (festivals, rituals, etc.) in the light of the Word of God. This is a very time-consuming but necessary and important process. Many Christians, for example, would like to continue, but are at the same time uncertain about, celebrating the various Chinese festivals. Many, too, know of the need to remove idols from their midst but few know exactly why. This is not healthy as it leads to the fallacy of people removing idols out of fear of becoming spiritually oppressed, rather than as an act of worship and commitment to God. As we examine the socio-cultural and religious backgrounds of the various Chinese festivals and practices, let us lay aside our bias and be open to explore the issues, holding firmly to the authority of the Word of God. This means that we retain that which is not contrary to it; reject in obedience all that is; and allow our conscience to determine how we might individually respond to and proceed with areas that are open to interpretation.

Chapter 2
Chinese Religious Beliefs

Chinese Religion

Interestingly, there is no major indigenous Chinese religion. To begin with, Buddhism is not indigenous to China, being an "import" from India. As such, one will find many similarities between Buddhism and Hinduism. In fact, if one were to visit Laos, a predominantly Buddhist country, and view some of its monuments, one would find that the Buddhist images there resemble very strikingly the images in the Hindu religious epic, the *Ramayana*. So, might the monkey god of ancient Chinese mythology be a parallel image of *Hanuman*,[2] the monkey king of Hindu mythology?

Next, an examination of Daoism shows that it did not start out as a religion per se, but as a system of philosophical thought; the same may be said of Confucianism. Basically, that which ruled the day for the Chinese was tribal folk religion in which each tribe worshipped its own provincial, city or village deities. These deities gained greater prominence during the *Shang* Dynasty, and as a result of migration (see section on Shenism).

Confucianism

The founder of this movement was *Kung Fu Tze* (551-479 BC), of which "Confucius" is the Latin transliteration.

Philosophical and Doctrinal Basis

In his teachings, Confucius did not emphasize the spiritual aspects of life. This arose from his perspective that if one could not even deal with the earthly life, one should not bother about the heavenly. (A saying oft attributed to Confuciusm is: If we know not life, why worry about death.) This is not to say that Confucius did not believe in the supernatural. He simply chose to focus on the here-and-now factor of the human life. Confucius was basically a humanist in that he believed in the human capacity and ability, advocating that all humans are by nature good. He believed that the behaviour and character of an individual are strongly influenced and shaped by the environment. Confucius taught that, though born good, humans end up corrupt when their minds are clouded by wrong thoughts and ideas fed by the environment. For example, if a pair of twins is separated at birth and raised in different environments, the twins will grow up quite differently, picking up either the good or bad habits of their environment. Should the father of one of the twins teach him to lie, steal and cheat, he will grow up a liar, thief and cheat. The contention, therefore, is that while we may be born with a good and pure nature, the environment around us corrupts and ultimately leads us astray.

For Confucius, the saving grace lies in the fact that we are good by nature. As such, we may become good again by cleaning up our minds, that is to say, by filling our minds with right thoughts that would ultimately result in the right actions. If you think the right thoughts, you will manifest the right behaviour and be saved. Hence the emphasis on being educated in the past and its wisdom, as well as in human and social relationships (see Figure 1: The Four Cardinal Virtues and the Five Cardinal Relationships). It is held that abiding by the Four Cardinal Virtues and the Five Cardinal Relationships will uncloud our minds, thus enabling us to perceive and be translated into the spiritual. Emphasizing the importance of the Four Cardinal Virtues, Confucianism also maintained the necessity of keeping the Five Cardinal Relationships in their right order. First is that between ruler and subject, followed by the relationships between father and son, husband and wife, and siblings and friends, in descending order.

Biblical Approach: Logical as the idea that one is conditioned towards evil by the environment sounds (compare with contem-

Figure 1: The Four Cardinal Virtues and the Five Cardinal Relationships

The Four Cardinal Virtues	The Five Cardinal Relationships
1. To be loyal to the ruler or state	1. Between ruler (state) and subject
2. To be filial to one's parents	2. Between father and son
3. To be kind to people	3. Between husband and wife
4. To be faithful to one's friends	4. Between older and younger brothers
	5. Between friends

1. The family unit is viewed as the key to a successful and united nation.
2. Filial piety is viewed as the greatest of all virtues (community and family before self).

porary research into behavioural science), it is not exactly biblical. There is truth and biblical basis in the need for our minds to be renewed and transformed (Romans 12:2). The biblical starting point, however, is not the mind but our very human nature, which as a result of the fall of man (Genesis 3) is sinful (Romans 5:12,14; 1 Corinthians 15:22). Confucius was right to believe that we need a pure nature in order to transform our minds. His mistake was to assume that all are born with this pure sinless nature. Our sinful nature is affirmed when we look at our children who, without being taught, know how to get angry and throw tantrums, or lie to cover up their mistakes.

As believers, we hold to the teaching that all are born with a sinful nature (Genesis 3), a bondage from which we need to be delivered. Through His death and resurrection, Jesus Christ broke our bondage to this sinful nature (John 3:16; Romans 5:17), making us new creations in Him (2 Corinthians 5:17).

In our new life, we are sanctified daily as we are taught and grow in the ways of God, being transformed more and more into the image of God by the renewing and transformation of our minds (Romans 12:2) under the guidance and empowering of the Holy Spirit (John 15:26,27; 16:7-14). Training the mind, therefore, is important for the spiritual renewal of our lives. The starting point, however, is not the training of our minds through self-effort (Ephesians 2:1-9), but through the saving grace of Christ, followed by the empowering of the Holy Spirit.

Is Confucius a Deity, and Confucianism a Religion?

Confucianism is not a religion, but a philosophy of life. In certain quarters, however, Confucius has been raised to the level of deity and is oft viewed by some to be the god of education.

There is a two-fold reason for this. First, is the development of ancestral worship, under which Confucius was revered and honoured to the point of him being viewed as a deity. Second, is the historical fact that an emperor of China, convinced of the importance and worth of Confucius' teachings, ordered a temple dedicated to the worship of Confucius to be built in each major town in China.

Biblical Approach: If Confucius himself were still alive today, he would probably be the first to state quite emphatically that he is no god and that his teachings are not meant to form the basis of a religion. For Christians, Confucius is simply a human being and his teachings, while of some value, need to be brought under the authority of the Word of God.

Buddhism

Buddhism started in India and spread throughout China around the first century BC. Its beginning revolved around *Siddharttha Gautama* (563-483 BC), a prince, who at birth was prophesied to be the saviour of the world. His father, the king, fearful that the prophecy might be true, purposed to keep *Gautama* cut off from the world outside the palace. Nonetheless, when *Gautama* grew up, he managed to sneak out of the palace one day and was appalled by the depth of poverty and suffering that he saw among the common folk. Faced with and unable to change this reality, *Gautama* renounced his life as a prince. Leaving the palace, he settled under a tree to meditate on life. It is held that through the course of his meditation, he achieved enlightenment concerning life and all its cares.

Theological and Doctrinal Basis

Buddhists believe that everyone has a Buddha-like nature in them — very much like the New Age movement, which holds that every person has the potential to be a god. Thus, there is no Supreme God and everyone is equally a part of the life force of the universe. In Buddhism creation is the result of the five elements of fire, metal, wood, water and earth being linked together by secondary causes. As there is no belief in a Supreme God, this creation of the earth and humanity is thus without purpose or plan, which is as good as saying that creation is the result of a "big bang". The goal of Buddhism is nirvana, the state of enlightenment whereby one sees through all life and is, therefore, released to live a tranquil life free from the demands and desires of existence, becoming one with the Ultimate (the life force of the universe). The chief idea is not primarily one of abstinence, but enlightenment. The following story illustrates this point.

There were two monks who came to a stream and met a lady who was trying to get across the stream without getting her feet wet. The older monk said to the lady, "Climb on my back and I will carry you across." The younger monk was terribly shocked to hear this, but kept quiet and walked on. After crossing the river, the older monk let the lady down and the monks continued their journey. As they walked on, the older monk noticed that his companion appeared troubled and asked what was troubling him. Unable to control himself any longer, the younger monk said, "Master, our teaching advocates that we should abstain from lust yet you, my master, carried this lady on your back across the stream." Interestingly, the master said, "My dear disciple, I carried the lady across the stream and then left her there. You, however, have continued to carry this lady in your thoughts despite us having travelled all this distance."

Though it may be the perception of many who seek to practise Buddhism or who are simply onlookers, abstinence is not the solution for the Buddhist. What is advocated is the pursuit of enlightenment, a pursuit that may be achieved by keeping the Four Noble Truths and the Noble Eight-fold Path. It is taught in the Four Noble Truths that all existence is suffering (*dukha*). For someone like *Gautama* who had lived in a palace with its luxuries to suddenly encounter poverty, it is natural to view all life as suffering. The teaching then follows that all suffering is the result of you and I. That is, human beings cause their own suffering because of their insatiable desire (*tanha*) for more and more things. To bring an end to the suffering, their *tanha* must be illuminated and this is achieved by following the Noble Eight-fold Path.

The Noble Eight-fold Path advocates a *right view* of the Four Noble Truths. That is to say, one must understand that everything is suffering and that suffering is the result of our own desires.

Figure 2: The Four Noble Truths and the Noble Eight-fold Path

The Four Noble Truths	The Noble Eight-fold Path
1. All existence is *dukka* (suffering). 2. *Dukka* is due to *tanha* (desire/craving). 3. To bring an end to *dukka*, our *tanha* must be illuminated. 4. Illumination is achieved through following the Noble Eight-fold Path.	1. Right view 2. Right mental attitude 3. Right speech 4. Right action 5. Right livelihood 6. Right effort 7. Right mindfulness 8. Right contemplation

Along with this, one must have a *right mental attitude* where no extremes are held, and peace and perfection sought. The Path also advocates honesty (*right speech*) and proper motives for all we do (*right action*). It teaches that one should not steal, but rather work for a living (*right livelihood*), with the correct mental attitude towards all aspects of life so that there is no indifference (*right effort*). In addition, there is to be at all times, a correct recollection (*right mindfulness*) and meditation (*right contemplation*) of the Four Noble Truths.

Biblical Approach: As believers, we do not hold to the idea that all creation, including humanity, simply came into being without purpose and plan. The existence of each and every aspect of creation was planned for by God and accounted as good (Genesis 1 and 2), which gives purpose to our continued existence and pursuit of the future. It is also our belief that all human beings are finite created beings without any god-nature. The "enlightenment" or "illumination" of our desires is important, but the necessary starting point is our salvation in Christ which sets us free from our bondage to sin (John 3:16; Romans 5:17) and subsequently empowers us with the Holy Spirit to live a life free from materialistic self-seeking. We may not achieve *nirvana* by seeking to illuminate our desire via the pursuit of the Four Noble Truths and the Noble Eight-fold Path in our own strength and ability. This is because no one is good or able enough, in and of his own strength and effort, to purchase salvation for himself. Salvation comes to us purely by faith (in Christ) through grace and not by works (Galatians 2:16; Ephesians 2:1-9). By believing in and turning to Jesus Christ, Christians receive immediate salvation and full assurance of a place in heaven.

Theravada and Mahayana Schools of Buddhism

Two major schools of thought in the Buddhist religion are the Mahayana and Theravada schools of Buddhism. The Mahayana is called the Greater School and the Theravada the Lesser School. The Theravada School was the first to be founded and is alternatively known as the Older School, while the Mahayana School that came later is known as the Younger School. In Theravada Buddhism, it is held that only monks can practise the Noble Eight-fold Path. Everyone may have knowledge of the Noble Eight-fold Path but only monks may effectively practise it to achieve enlightenment. In this scenario, a person must first accumulate enough merit in his previous life so as to be reincarnated (passing away from one life to be reborn into another) as a monk in the present one. This enables him to practise the Noble Eight-fold Path and potentially achieve *nirvana*. It does not take a lot for us to realize that this line of thought effectively cuts off many Buddhists from achieving *nirvana*. Say, for example, we have a million Buddhists living in a particular locale and only one per cent of them are monks. That means that only one in a hundred may practise the Noble Eight-fold Path and potentially achieve *nirvana*. This is not a very good percentage by any means and the people who founded the Mahayana school may well have thought the same. It is the teaching of the Mahayana School that, apart from the monks, everyone else could also practise the Noble Eight-fold Path and share equally in the chance to achieve *nirvana*.

Biblical Approach: Christians do not believe in reincarnation. Even if we were to entertain the idea of reincarnation, the system leaves us with absolutely no assurance of salvation. This is simply because we do not know how much merit one requires for salvation or even how much merit one has already accumulated for each reincarnation. We have only one life to live, and laid before each of us is the invitation to draw near to God and receive from Him eternal life as we turn to Jesus Christ to confess our sins and accept Him into our hearts (John 3:16). The time to make a decision with regard to our salvation is today, not after we are dead and gone for we will have no second chance (Hebrews 9:27).

Daoism

The acclaimed founders of Daoism were *Lao Tze* (604-524 BC) and *Zhuang Tze* (369-286 BC). *Lao Tze* founded the philosophical school of Daoist thought (*Dao Jia*), which emphasized wisdom and seniority. This school of thought focused on the social dimension of life, advocating that a person may achieve immortality through the pursuit of wisdom. Thus, seniority is highly regarded and the elderly revered for the wealth of knowledge and wisdom accumulated in their lifetime. *Zhuang Tze* founded the spiritual school of Daoist belief (the *Dao Jiao*). This school emphasized the spiritual dimension of life and focused on the use of alchemy and magic to achieve a longer life span and immortality. In many Chinese period dramas on television, we often see emperors asking certain priests to brew a pill of immortality for them. This idea is drawn from the belief that one may live forever by consuming the pill of immortality concocted from various substances (for example, cinnabar, gum of the peach tree and ginseng) or through the performance of certain rites and rituals.

Philosophical and Doctrinal Beliefs

Daoism advocates that all parts of the cosmos belong to one

organic whole (that is, the *Dao*). As such, harmony and order must be maintained at all times — in the individual psyche, in every aspect of social life and in the entire cosmos — for all creation to live and function perfectly. All that exists, including humans, is derived from the *Dao* and each has its correct place in it. Daoism teaches that our inner spiritual disharmony with the *Dao* is the essential missing ingredient of true religion and right living. To live a good life and be at peace with the universe, one needs to be in harmony with the *Dao*.

The *Dao* is considered to be the very source and nature of all creation. It is nameless and indescribable, and it is taught that if one can describe the *Dao*, that which has been described is not the *Dao*. The *Dao*, however, is not held to be a supreme god or being. It is simply the universal life force. Everything is a result of the *Dao* and everything leads to the *Dao*. Every living being or thing has the *Dao* within it and is part of the *Dao*. This makes every living thing, be it animal or vegetable, inextricably connected to the *Dao*. One must not, therefore, act against the harmonious flow of nature. To do so would create chaos in the whole (*Dao*) and cause great imbalance. An example would be when a person dies; for death brings disharmony upon the whole. Certain rites and rituals would then have to be conducted to restore this broken harmony.

Biblical Approach: As Christians, we hold no belief that one may attain longevity or immortality through the cultivation of wisdom (as advocated by the *Dao Jia*) or through the use of alchemy and the practice of certain rites and rituals. The Bible is very clear that no one may attain immortality by the works of his own hands (Ephesians 2:1-9); it is possible only by the grace and mercy of God (John 3:16). We also do not hold to the Daoist teaching on how the world was created. Doing so would disregard the clear teaching of the Bible that all things were created out of nothing (*ex nihilo*) by the word and will of God (Genesis 1:1ff; John 1:1ff). Advocating a Daoist view of the creation of the world would also leave us with a very uncertain present and future. If no one has planned our birth, there can be no concrete purpose for our current existence, nor is there anything to look forward to in our future. The Bible clearly teaches that our existence is not by accident, but according to the plan of God (Genesis 1 and 2). The Daoist view also negates any personal responsibility for sin, a perspective contrary to the teaching of the Bible (Romans 3:23).

Shenism

Shenism is a very *Singlish*[3] term derived by adding "ism" to the Chinese word *shen* (which means deity or immortal); a term that I first heard used by one of my Bible college lecturers. It was coined to refer to the indigenous tribal folk religions of China.

Historical Development and Traditional Beliefs

Folk religion was commonly practised in various parts of China and came to prominence during the *Shang* Dynasty (1751-1122 BC). It also became widespread as people migrated and travelled from city to city and from province to province for work and other reasons. As these people moved about, some would bring along their local village, city or provincial deities, which might then be introduced to their friends and colleagues, or even to strangers whom they met. Thus, we may find today people from one Chinese province or dialect group worshipping a deity that was traditionally from another province or dialect group, making this local deity the "property" of everyone. Practitioners of Shenism believe in a powerful and real spirit world filled with spirits (see Figure 3: Categories of *Shen*) whose behaviour is patterned on human activities. The more powerful spirits are thought to have the ability to influence human lives and control human activities. In the practice of Shenism, the pragmatic Chinese will believe in and worship anything that can prosper and bless them.

Biblical Approach: Believers are not to get involved in Shenism because though the Bible does speak of evil spirits, it does not teach such a perception of the spirit world. The Bible tells us that

Figure 3: Categories of *Shen*

Spirit beings of heaven	For example, *Tien Gong*; star spirits; wind, rain, thunder and lightning spirits
Spirit beings of earth	For example, *Tu Di Gong*; wood and fire deity; waterway or water spirit
Household deities	For example, the kitchen god; god of fame; god of prosperity; god of longevity
Temple deities	For example, *Na Cha*; the monkey god; the nine-emperor gods
Good and evil spirits	Good spirits are believed to be local deities with influence on daily life, while evil spirits are believed to be the deceased who are unwilling to let go of life on earth

there is only one true God over all (Deuteronomy 4:35; 32:39; 1 Corinthians 8:4), and all other "gods" are but pale imitations brought about by demonic spirits (1 Chronicles 16:26; Psalm 96:5).[4]

Chinese Religious Practice Today

Indigenous to China, Confucianism is a system of philosophical thought, not a religion. However, through the years, its founder, Confucius, has been revered and often raised to the status of a deity by the common people. Daoism also began as a philosophical school of thought (advocating the thoughts of *Lao Tze* and *Zhuang Tze*). Though this is the only indigenous "religion" of the Chinese today, we do not know when it took on the characteristics and status of a religion. Buddhism, on the other hand, is not an indigenous religion of China, having been introduced to China from India around the first century AD. During the *Ming* dynasty, religious thinkers such as *Lin Chao-En* (1517-1598) sought to harmonize the three major Chinese beliefs of Confucianism, Buddhism and Daoism into one major religion by drawing upon the best elements of the three. The effectiveness of this attempted synthesis may be seen in the fact that very few Chinese today would think it strange to be a Confucianist, a Buddhist and a Daoist all at the same time.

The bulk of Chinese religious practice today is an amalgam of these three major religious and philosophical streams of thought plus Shenism (traditional folk religion). For example, during a Chinese funeral, should Chinese traditional rites be desired, those who traditionally believe in and perform such rites would be the *Dao Jiao* priests. Today, you would also find Buddhists performing rites for the deceased despite the fact that traditional, classical, proper Buddhists do not believe in them. For traditional Buddhists, the emphasis is on achieving enlightenment through meditation, not rites and rituals. There are, therefore, very few people who practise pure Buddhism or Daoism or the like. Many of those engaged in Chinese religious practices today lack a real depth of knowledge of the basic tenets of their practices. Most continue in them not because they know or understand what they are doing, but because it is a tradition. A practice may be continued as an act of filial piety and with a pragmatic desire for blessings — to please, so our ancestors may bless, or to appease lest our ancestors get angry and allow disasters to befall us.

Of late, there has been a resurgence of interest among the young in Buddhism in Singapore. One reason for this may be attributed to the fact that the Buddhists have changed their philosophy of ministry. Where the Buddhist sutra has been used and taught only in Sanskrit in the past, it is today being explained in the vernacular (that is, in the native tongue of the local people). This is a draw for many young people from families traditionally associated with Chinese religious practices, but who are not versed in Sanskrit, as it is easier for them to relate to and accept the teachings of Buddhism. Another draw is the holding of classes on career development and stress management, along with the establishment of cell groups and the singing of choruses (some of which have Christian tunes).

General Comments: Christians have for centuries advocated the need to present the Gospel and the teaching of the Word of God in the vernacular, as it is important for people to understand what they read and hear. There is no special sacred language in which the worship of God is to be communicated (be it Latin, Greek, Aramaic, Hebrew or Sanskrit).

The Main Events

Chapter 3
Festivals of the Living

A General Observation

The main events in the Chinese calendar, apart from the wedding, are divided into two categories. One is called "Festivals of the Living" and the other "Festivals of the Dead". The former are festivals that have nothing directly to do with ancestral worship, though offerings to ancestors may be made during the course of the celebrations. For example, during *Chun Jie* (Chinese New Year), the ancestral altar is cleaned and fresh offerings (fruit, chicken, etc.) made. The latter festivals, on the other hand, are specifically targeted at remembering the dead. As we go along, you will notice that a majority of the festivals tie in with the lunar calendar as well as the harvest season. This is similar to the festivals recorded in the Bible, many of which were linked to the lunar calendar and the harvest season.

Chun Jie

This festival, normally celebrated in February, is tied to the arrival of spring. Following a cold dark winter, the arrival of spring — when everything starts to grow again and birds and animals return — was traditionally welcomed with a celebration. Most in tropical lands would not appreciate this change in climate. Even those today who live in lands with such climatic changes may not appreciate the arrival of spring as much as their forebears as they have access to heaters for warmth and supermarkets for food. In ancient days, when there was no electricity and winters were cold and dark, the arrival of spring was a major occasion for celebration. It was in this context that *Chun Jie*, also known as the Spring Festival, Lunar New Year or Chinese New Year, was celebrated. It was the beginning of spring and a time to celebrate the new life that was about to spring forth.

Mythological History

The myth surrounding the celebration of *Chun Jie* tells of the existence in ancient days of a terrifying beast named *nian* (a Chinese word meaning "year"). This beast slept throughout the year, waking up only once for a short period of time. Having hibernated for most of the year, it would naturally wake up hungry and would roam the land seeking whom it might devour. Though fearful of the beast, the people of the land soon discovered that it was afraid of bright lights, loud noise and the colour red. They then sought to defend themselves. Thus, on the eve of the beast rousing from hibernation, they gathered as family groups to find safety in numbers. All the lights in their homes were switched on to ward off the beast and firecrackers were kept at hand to scare it away. They also wore red and hung red cloth and lanterns over their doorposts. As added protection for their children, small red packets were given out.

General Comments: Note how the ideas of family gatherings on the eve of *Chun Jie*; the importance of the colour red; the giving of *ang pows* (small red envelopes / packets with money inside); and the firing of firecrackers have been interwoven into the myth. There is, of course, no basis to this myth as the real root of *Chun Jie* is the celebration of the arrival of spring.

Traditional Practices and Superstitions

There are many traditional practices associated with *Chun Jie*, of which we will mention only a few. The most prominent tradition is the reunion dinner held on its eve. Most, working far from home and who would not normally bother about family gatherings, make a serious effort to be home for this gathering. In some countries in South-East Asia, for example, one would often book the air passage home six months or more in advance to ensure a seat on the plane. Related to the reunion dinner, have you ever wondered why so much food is cooked for it? During a reunion dinner some years ago, one of my siblings asked my late mother why there was so much food on the table when we knew that we could not possibly finish eating it all. She said, "You are not supposed to finish eating all the food, for having leftovers from the reunion meal means the family will continue to enjoy abundance (for example, food and money) in the New Year."

Another traditional practice with superstitious overtones is the spring-cleaning of the home. While most simply desire to have their home in the nicest possible state for visits by friends, many also believe in a supernatural significance to the act. The belief advocates that one may clean the house up till midnight on the eve of *Chun Jie*, but must thereafter avoid sweeping the floor for the duration of the celebration. Sweeping up to the eve of *Chun Jie* helps remove bad luck, but if done during the days of celebration, it would simply sweep away all the good luck that the New Year brings. After spring-cleaning, the home is decorated with various symbols of blessing, luck and well wishes, of which the following are some examples:

Figure 4: Some *Chun Jie* Symbols and their Significance

***Chun Jie* Symbols**	**Significance**
1. Pussy willow	1. Longevity
2. Kumquat and mandarin oranges	2. Luck and prosperity
3. Plum blossom	3. Purity and honesty
4. Tossing the *yu sheng* (raw fish) salad	4. Fish for abundance, pomelo for luck, crackers for pile of gold, etc.
5. Auspicious words on red paper	5. Wishes of blessing and abundance

Traditionally, *Chun Jie* celebrations begin with the feeding of *nian gao* (a sweet and sticky cake) to the kitchen god on the twenty-third day of the twelfth lunar month. This is to bribe the kitchen god so that in his annual reporting to the emperor of heaven, he would have nothing but nice things to say about the family. On the first day of *Chun Jie*, the young will rise early to wish their elders well, and receive well wishes and *ang pows* in return. The family would then change into new clothes (meant to symbolize the wish for blessing and bounty in the year ahead) and prepare themselves to receive, or set off to visit their relatives, neighbours and friends.

Biblical Approach: The reunion dinner is a good tradition to keep, especially since most of us are often so busy with our own activities that we hardly have time to gather as one family and catch up with one another. We must not, however, buy into the superstition of ensuring that there is too much food for the family to finish. The act does not ensure that we will have plenty of food on the table in the coming year. As believers, we look to God for the provision of our daily needs and it is His promise that He knows our needs and will always provide for us (Matthew 6:25-34). Spring-cleaning in preparation for the celebration of *Chun Jie* is an acceptable practice, but do not get caught up in the superstitious belief that if you sweep the floor during *Chun Jie*, you will lose all your blessings and good fortune. It is both our hard work (Proverbs 15:19) and the blessing of God that provide us with our daily necessities, not superstitious practices.

The same is to be said for the new clothes that we buy and the auspicious decorations we put up in our homes. They express our hopes and wishes, but we must be careful not to read more into them. To be upset should one not wear new clothes or if the decorations are put up in the wrong place or manner[1] is to fall into the trap of superstitious belief. The giving of *ang pows* by elders to their unmarried children is another tradition for which there is no Christian objection. It is, however, left entirely to the individual to decide if he wants to do this. What about the practice of feeding the kitchen god with *nian gao*? Though it does mention the presence of household idols (Genesis 31:19), the Bible is clear in teaching that these idols are powerless (Psalm 115:4-8). Believers should thus hold no belief in the existence or efficacy of a kitchen god.

In itself, there is nothing wrong with Chinese believers celebrating *Chun Jie*, embracing it as part of their cultural heritage (treating it as a spring festival in its original purpose holds little meaning for many today). We must, however, choose between keeping the components of *Chun Jie* that are acceptable and rejecting those that are not. For example, it is worthwhile for us to maintain the observance of the reunion dinner. We must not, though, engage in the various superstitious practices related to auspicious decorations or food. Neither are we to participate in the act of cleaning the ancestral altar and setting fresh food offerings before it with prayers, a common practice during *Chun Jie* for those engaged in ancestral worship.

Duan Wu Jie

Celebrated on the fifth day of the fifth lunar month (normally around July), *Duan Wu Jie* is also known as the Dragon Boat Festival.

Historical Development

This festival commemorates the patriotism and literary talent of *Qu Yuan* of the kingdom of *Chu* (around 300 BC). *Qu Yuan* was a scholar and a loyal subject of the kingdom of *Chu* who, when told that his country had been conquered by the army of the kingdom of *Qin*, was so upset that he threw himself into the *Mi Luo* river. When the locals heard that *Qu Yuan*, who was well liked and respected, had committed suicide, they rushed to the river in an attempt to save him. They dredged the river with hooks to try to find his body but to no avail. Afraid that fish would eat his body, they then wrapped and threw rice into the river in the hope that this, instead of the body, would be eaten. From the efforts of these people, we have as celebratory components today, the dragon boat races (dredging of the river) and *zhong zi* or rice dumplings (the wrapped rice thrown into the river to feed the fish).

Biblical Approach: Dragon boat races and rice dumplings are mere signs that help people to remember *Qu Yuan* and his story. There are no religious or superstitious connotations attached to the eating of *zhong zi* (rice dumplings), but what of the dragon boat races? First, most Christians would have no objections to these races if, while all else remained the same, the "dragon" head at the prow is removed. The objection lies, therefore, not with the race per se, but with the representation of a dragon at the head of the boat. (For a discussion on dragons, see Appendix A.) Second, it is common practice for rites to be held when commissioning a new dragon boat to "open the eyes of the dragon" whose head is at the prow. This is an ancient practice not confined to the Chinese, as the ability of the figure at the prow to protect and lead a ship and her crew to safety is an old maritime belief. Such rites and beliefs are, however, contrary to our Christian belief and believers should have nothing to do with such events and practices.

As the root of this festival is the commemoration of the loyalty and sacrifice of a patriot, there need be no Christian objection to its celebration. In addition, it has never been claimed that *Qu Yuan* is now a *shen* (deity). The celebration of this festival can be a means of teaching people about patriotism and loyalty to the nation. This is an important lesson, as many today are becoming far too individualistic, promoting a "me-mine-and-I-come-first-over-all-else" mindset and perspective. In such an environment, it is good to remember people like *Qu Yuan*, dedicated and committed as he was to his country.

Zhong Qiu Jie

Zhong Qiu Jie, also known as the Mid-Autumn Festival or the

Moon Cake Festival, is celebrated on the fifteenth day of the eighth lunar month, normally around September.

Mythological Basis and Historical Significance

This festival centres around the myth of *Hou Yi* and his wife *Chang-E*. The story goes that in ancient China, there was a time when 10 deities (children of the emperor of heaven) came down to earth from heaven to play. They were so radiant that the people on earth perceived them as 10 bright, hot suns. As they had such a fun time on earth, the deities were in no hurry to return to heaven. In their enjoyment though, they failed to realize that they were scorching the earth with their heat and causing a great drought and famine. In response to this calamity, the emperor of China decreed that the person who could deliver the land from this plague would marry his daughter, the Princess *Chang-E*, and rule the country. Many tried unsuccessfully until *Hou Yi* came along.

Hou Yi, an archer, began shooting down the suns one by one, with each falling to earth in the form of a raven, till there remained only one. The emperor kept his promise and *Hou Yi* and *Chang-E* were soon married. When *Hou Yi* took over as ruler of the land, however, he proved to be a wicked ruler, a dictator and a despot who treated the people very badly. He wanted to live forever and instructed his priests to make a pill of immortality for him. When the pill was finally produced, *Chang-E*, sad that her husband was a bad ruler and realizing that the people would suffer greatly should he live forever, took the pill and ate it. *Hou Yi* was very angry and wanted to kill her, but because *Chang-E* had taken the pill of immortality, she became as light as a fairy, floated up into the sky and landed on the moon. In this way did *Chang-E* become the lady in the moon and the basis for the celebration of this festival.

The historical significance of this festival lies in a plot by *Zhu Yuan Zhang* in the fourteenth century to overthrow the *Yuan* dynasty, a task he ultimately accomplished. In this uprising, to avoid detection, rebel communication was baked into and passed along in moon cakes. Apart from the myth of the lady in the moon and this historical significance, there is no firm data on the origin of this festival. With its focus on the moon, however, one might not be too far wrong to surmise that it probably arose from the practice of worshipping the moon. Moon cakes (reflecting the abode of *Chang-E*) and the carrying of lanterns (because the festival is primarily celebrated at night when the moon is out) are the main symbols of this festival. Note that the use of moon cakes as a component of the festival to commemorate the sacrifice of *Chang-E* was already in place before their use as a means of hiding rebel communication.

Biblical Approach: Is there any religious significance to the eating of moon cakes and the carrying of lanterns? Some have argued that these activities might communicate the mistaken notion that we are engaged in the worship of *Chang-E* or give the false impression that we condone it. The issue here concerns what we communicate both verbally and non-verbally about the acceptability of this event. Thus, we must take into consideration the long-term ramifications (of potential converts thinking that they may become Christians and still celebrate such festivals) and not simply the short-term gain (that it attracts the immediate attention of many).

While *Zhong Qiu Jie* has an element of commemorating the overthrow of the *Yuan* dynasty by *Zhu Yuan Zhang*, it remains primarily a festival based on a mythological belief in the lady in the moon, *Chang-E*. This is amply attested to by the fact that there is no mention of *Zhu Yuan Zhang* during any celebration of this festival. The focus remains on the lady in the moon. In light of this, Christians should have nothing to do with this festival.

An Alternative: Attempts have been made in recent years to give this festival a Christian basis by focusing on a celebration of creation (of which the moon is a part) and on how Christ has made our lives complete (like the fully rounded moon).[2] Personally, I find this to be a rather forced argument. If asked to choose, I find that *Duan Wu Jie* is a better festival for believers to celebrate as its focus on loyalty and patriotism does not contradict the teachings of God. This clear focus also removes any need for us to think up some explanation for organizing a Christian gathering during this or any other festival.

CHAPTER 4

FESTIVALS OF THE DEAD

A General Observation

The following festivals, namely *Qing Ming Jie, Zhong Yuan Jie* and *Chong Yang Jie,* are particularly geared towards remembrance of the dead and ancestral worship.

Qing Ming Jie

This festival is celebrated in spring, when plants begin to bloom again after winter, in April, in relation to the end of the second moon or the beginning of the third moon of the Chinese lunar calendar.

Historical Development

This festival is popularly associated with *Jie Zi Dui* (600 BC), who was a popular and well-known scholar. The emperor of *Jing, Wen Kong,* had wanted to recruit *Jie Zi Dui* to serve in the imperial court, but *Jie Zi Dui* declined, as he did not want to get caught up in the corruption of the court. So he withdrew to a mountain retreat and lived in seclusion to concentrate on his studies and meditation. The emperor tried time and time again to persuade him to serve the imperial court but *Jie Zi Dui* was adamant. One day, the emperor got so angry and upset that he passed the order that should *Jie Zi Dui* reject the offer once more, the army was to set fire to the mountain. When *Jie Zi Dui* still turned down the emperor, the order was carried out and *Jie Zi Dui* perished in the fire. On learning of the death of *Jie Zi Dui*, the emperor regretted his actions and, out of penance and remembrance, declared that none were to light a fire on the anniversary of the scholar's death. As a result, this festival also came to be known as the Cold Food Festival, as there was no fire during its celebration for the preparation of warm food. Over time, this festival grew to be a time to remember loved ones who had passed away.

Biblical Approach: On the face of it, as this festival does not of itself bear any religious significance, Christians need not have any inhibitions about observing it. It is, after all, right for us to remember our dearly departed. There are, however, other considerations to take into account.

Traditional Observances and Practices

Qing Ming Jie is a time when the Chinese remember their departed and make a special effort to visit tombs, columbariums (for those whose loved ones have been cremated) and temples (where many today may leave the ashes or ancestral tablets of their departed relatives). It is an occasion for the whole family to visit and clean up the place where the remains of their ancestors have been interred. For those who do so, the time is made more meaningful by a recapitulation, to the next generation/s, of the life and contributions of the ancestor. The offering of food, joss sticks and paper money is a common feature of this visit.

Biblical Approach: The debate rages with regard to the participation of Christians in these visits. The accusation is that by not visiting the place where the remains of their ancestor/s are interred, believers are turning their backs on their family and showing a lack of filial piety. The heart of the issue is not the visit or its timing during *Qing Ming Jie*, but the acts of ancestral worship (for example, making offerings of food and incense) that take place as part and parcel of these visits. What if the remains of the departed are in a temple? As believers, we need not fear stepping into a temple because we have Christ in us, the sovereign Lord by our side. Nonetheless, let us not be complacent or brash and, in the process, open ourselves to spiritual attack. It is best to avoid such visits. As the remains of our dearly beloved may now be interred in fairly neutral environs, I recommend that this be done wherever possible.

Are we insensitive and lacking in filial piety if we do not participate in *Qing Ming Jie*? It is argued that observing this festival helps to show skeptical non-believers that Christians do remember and commemorate the dead. Some Christian congregations, therefore, encourage their members to visit the tombs of their ancestors during *Qing Ming Jie* (a time to remember the departed and not a time for ancestral worship per se) as a Christian witness, to show that they are still part of the family. However, due to the common practice of making food offerings and worship activities, abstaining from such visits during this festival might be in order. In doing so, we lay aside and separate ourselves from the idolatrous practice of ancestral worship and bear witness to non-believers of our commitment to God. It has been argued that believers may simply stand aside and not participate in the presentation of offerings. This is true enough. However, what happens should we be present at the tomb and refuse to participate in the rituals? Would that not also lead to unhappiness and accusations of a lack of filial piety?

The decision, ultimately, rests with our individual conscience. As individuals, we have to make up our own minds. The person looking to make such a decision should consider:

1. The context and the duties demanded (for example, visitation and cleaning of the tomb, as opposed to the presentation of offerings); and
2. The circumstances and the motive (for example, remembrance and witness, or fear of retribution and desire for blessings from the deceased).

(See Appendix B for a fuller discussion on this issue.)

An Alternative: If, as believers, we do not participate in *Qing Ming Jie*, how and what can we to do to show filial piety? In actual fact, the Christian calendar provides viable alternatives to this festival. Two days have been set apart for Christians to visit and clean up the places where the remains of their ancestors are interred: Good Friday (in April) and All Souls' Day (in November). Every Easter, memorial services are conducted at cemeteries and columbariums to commemorate our departed. Then, in November, there is a day called All Souls' Day, that follows after All Saints' Day, and this is the second time in the year that we remember our dearly departed. So, going purely by the number of festivals per year to remember the departed, Christians may be said to be more filial as we remember the departed on two separate occasions, whereas others do so only once.

Zhong Yuan Jie

This festival is usually celebrated around August, throughout the entire seventh lunar month, and is popularly known as the Hungry Ghost Festival. It demonstrates the concern in Chinese religious belief for the pitiable existence of souls not cared for by the living. It is especially dedicated to the *kui* (hungry ghosts) released from their abode in hell to roam the earth during this month.

Philosophical and Doctrinal Basis

In Daoism, the gates of hell are opened on the first day of the seventh lunar month. This allows the *kui* (uncared for spirits or spirits under judgement that are locked in hell) to roam the earth to eat their fill before being locked up for another year. The belief is that once the gates are opened, these *kui* will come out to look for food and if no one has prepared any offerings for them, they will go into homes to help themselves. Fearful of such visits, people are generally quick to make offerings to appease and ward off the hungry ghosts. Interestingly, the first day of the seventh lunar month was also the day the gates of the first temple in Jerusalem were first opened (2 Chronicles 7), and the day the Feast of Tabernacles commences (Leviticus 23:34; Nehemiah 8).

Biblical Approach: There is no biblical basis for the opening of the gates of hell for the *kui* to roam the earth once a year. The Bible is clear that once a person passes on from life on earth, he is held without parole in *Hades* / *Sheol* or the bosom of Abraham (Luke 16:22ff) to await judgement on the Last Day (Romans 14:10b; 2 Corinthians 5:10). Christians, therefore, are not to hold any belief in this festival. It is, however, interesting for us to note a contrasting parallel. For Christians, the first day of the seventh lunar month is a day of great rejoicing, a time when the gates of the temple in Jerusalem were opened and the blessings of the Lord poured out. In Revelation, the imagery is that of a river of the water of life flowing out from the throne of God (Ezekiel 47:1; Revelation 22:1ff). Whereas for many Chinese, it is a time of great fear as the gates of hell are thrown open and the *kui* are released to roam the earth.

Popular Association

Buddhists associate *Zhong Yuan Jie* with the myth of *Mu Lian*. The story goes that *Mu Lian* was a very filial son who, after the death of his mother, dreamt one night that she was in hell. In the dream, his mother appeared and said to him, "I am hungry, I am not being taken care of and am poorly treated." *Mu Lian* was so moved and touched by this dream that he decided to bring food down to hell to feed his mother. To do so, he had to endure many trials and difficulties in an attempt to gain favour from various gods. After much hardship, he ultimately reached hell and was "reunited" with his mother. This story is told to encourage filial piety towards parents and elders.

Biblical Approach: One of the 10 commandments of our Lord is that we honour our father and mother, that we might enjoy length of days on earth (Exodus 20:12). Filial piety towards our parents is, therefore, definitely encouraged by our Lord Jesus Christ (Matthew 15:1-9). There is, however, no basis to the myth of *Mu Lian*. In addition, no living human being may, by any means, descend into hell to visit a departed relative. Believers should in no way hold to or propagate this myth.

Related Events and Practices

As part of the celebrations of this festival, a *ge tai* (variety show) is often held, primarily to entertain the *kui* in the hope that when distracted or happy, they will not look for or disturb living beings. The first night of the *ge tai* is traditionally meant for the *kui* to attend. Another practice is to hold celebratory dinners, during which various items of luck and blessing will be auctioned off. Many would bid for these items in the hope and belief that they would, in the year ahead, bring prosperity to the owners. The most prized possession is a block of charcoal. This relates back to the myth of *Mu Lian*, where it is held that when *Mu Lian* finally reached hell, the buns he brought to feed his mother had turned into charcoal.

Biblical Approach: Believers are not to participate in any of the superstitious activities discussed above. This is not to say that we are participating in the festival should we simply stand in the crowd and enjoy the *ge tai* performances. Participation refers to our getting involved by making contributions towards the *ge tai* and dinners, bidding during the auctions, etc. We should not be involved in any of the superstitions surrounding the festival or buy into the fear that the *kui* would come haunting. In relation to the dinners, you might well ask if we could simply attend without engaging in the superstitious practices of the event. 1 Corinthians 10:21 clearly teaches us that we cannot partake of the table of our Lord and of the table of idols. As far as these celebratory dinners are concerned, this teaching applies. Basically, when people come together for such dinners, they are also celebrating and remembering a non-Scriptural and superstitious event. As such, believers should have nothing to do with these dinners.

A Time for Prayer

There is no cultural or spiritual value in believers celebrating *Zhong Yuan Jie*; it does nothing other than instil fear. The common belief that a lot more people die during this festival than at any other time is a cause of great fear. Believers should not buy into or propagate such a lie of the devil. We should, rather, rest secure in the knowledge and assurance of our salvation and victory in Christ (Romans 8:35-39). In addition, we must remember that the Bible does not teach that the gates of hell would or may be opened once a year for a month. Believers are not to participate in any way in this festival but should, instead, pray for the covering of our Lord to be over everyone. I encourage this because I believe that demonic activity increases during this month, not because the gates of hell are open, but because the devil knows that people believe they are. It is, therefore, a good time for the enemy to deceive and stir up even more fear, that people may be bound even more to their superstitions and superstitious practices. Believers should, therefore, pray more for their relatives and friends during *Zhong Yuan Jie*, that they may find peace and salvation in our Lord Jesus Christ and be set free from all their fears.

Chong Yang Jie

Chong Yang Jie, also known as the Double Ninth Festival, is normally celebrated around October, from the first to the ninth day of the ninth lunar month.

Historical and Religious Development

Chong Yang Jie was originally a celebration of autumn when, before the long winter set in, people paid their last visit to the tomb of their dearly departed. They would make offerings of food and winter clothing to the deceased to protect them from hunger and cold during the long winter. For some, this visit to the tomb also served as the last family outing before winter. There is a tale that relates why some (like people in Hong Kong) would climb mountains during the celebration of this festival. The story goes that there was once a farmer who dreamt that a great calamity would strike his farm and all in it. On waking up the next day, the farmer acted on this premonition and moved his whole family and livestock up to the mountains. True enough, the calamity struck but the farmer and all that belonged to him were saved. It is in remembrance of this tale that some today celebrate this festival by going mountain climbing.

Another aspect of this festival concerns the worship of a constellation of nine stars acknowledged as the deities *Jiu Huang Da Di* (the Nine Emperor Gods). Worshippers of the *Jiu Huang Da Di* would go to the seaside on the first day of the ninth lunar month to welcome these deities with nine sedan chairs decked in yellow. The colour yellow is meant to symbolize the mourning over Emperor *Chong Zhen*, the last emperor of the *Ming* dynasty who was overthrown by the Manchurians in 1644. After feasting the *Jiu Huang Da Di* for a week, worshippers would send them off, again at the seaside, on the ninth day. This festival is also known as the Vegetarian Festival because those celebrating it only partake of vegetarian meals for its duration, having fasted for a month before it began. No devotee is supposed to kill any living thing during this time; worshippers in Thailand also pierce their bodies, often with common everyday items like desk lamps, as an act of purification.[3]

Biblical Approach: For most people, having one last outing with the family is no longer relevant, with many continuing to enjoy outings during the winter months. It definitely has no relevance in a tropical country like Singapore. There is also no basis to keep this festival based on the tale of the farmer, as it is simply a tale. For Christians who hold no belief in the worship of the *Jiu Huang Da Di* or the need of the departed for winter clothes or food, there is no reason to celebrate this festival.

There is no biblical basis or cultural value in our keeping of this festival. As the primary emphasis of *Chong Yang Jie* is ancestral worship (the winter offerings) and the worship of the *Jiu Huang Da Di* (the Bible teaches such worship to be an act of idolatry in 1 Corinthians 10:20), Christians are to have nothing to do with the celebration of *Chong Yang Jie*.

General Evaluation

Generally speaking, it is acceptable for Christians to celebrate cultural and historical events — *Chun Jie* and *Duan Wu Jie*, for example — but we must not engage in any superstitious or religious practices associated with, and traditionally carried out during, the various festivals. For example, though there is no religious significance to the celebration of *Chun Jie*, it is common for people to make special offerings to their ancestors at this time. A clear line must be drawn between the historical and culturally acceptable, and the superstitious and religious which are absolutely unacceptable. A major difficulty in seeking to abstain from the practice of ancestral worship and its outward manifestations, however, is the pressure placed on a person — by parents, siblings, relatives and friends — to conform to the Chinese religious norm. No quick and easy answer may be given in this issue. The motive, however, for any choice made is very important and should always serve to glorify God.

Each individual must simply do as his conscience dictates, resting upon the assurance that if a genuine mistake is made, our Lord Jesus Christ will accept our heartfelt repentance and forgive us (1 John 1:9). As much as our Lord Jesus Christ freely forgives our failures, we must also learn to forgive ourselves. Should a wrong choice of action be taken, we must repent. Having done so and received our Lord's forgiveness, we should then seek to grow in our Christian life without fear or the stigma of having failed our Lord, for there is no condemnation in Christ (Romans 8:1ff). Those of us staying on the sidelines must learn not to be too quick in passing judgement on an individual for an apparent compromise of faith. Neither should we put someone struggling for a right response under the added bondage of fear of possible spiritual oppression or possession upon participation in questionable rites (the perfect love of God residing within us casts out all fear — 1 John 4:18).

Biblical Approach: A believer should disclose his conversion to Christianity to his parents as soon as possible. This would ensure that when a stand needs to be made, for example, over one's participation in funeral rites, family members would have had time to come to terms with the individual's new-found faith and the principles of the faith that he has to adhere to. We must endeavour to please God and make no compromise in our faith. Though this is not an easy task, it is one that we must be prepared to face; and we face it with the assurance of God's abiding presence and aid (John 16:7ff; Acts 4:8a; 1 Corinthians 10:13; 2 Corinthians 12:9).

Chapter 5
The Marriage Tradition

The Wedding Rite

In Chinese tradition, the wedding rite is the passage into maturity and adulthood. That is to say, a single person, regardless of age, is not considered a full-fledged adult unless and until he gets married. Traditional wedding arrangements and requirements vary from dialect group to dialect group. For example, while those belonging to the *Teochew* dialect group generally require the bride to leave her home before sunrise, with the inclusion of a suckling pig in the dowry a must, those from other dialect groups are not so stringent about these requirements. The custom of fetching the bride before sunrise was probably a very practical one as in ancient days, the bride may well live some distance from the groom. A groom would, therefore, have to rise early to fetch his bride if the marriage ceremony and celebrations were to be carried out within the same day. Over time, people imputed superstitious connotations to this practice, believing that the marriage procession must start off early to avoid any unpleasantness on the way. It was deemed inauspicious should anything bad be encountered on the road, for example, accidents, fights, etc.

In the old days, there was no National Registrar of Marriages. People, therefore, usually got married in the home before the family altar. The night before the wedding, the mother would comb the hair of the bride, proclaiming a word of blessing with each stroke of the comb. On the morning of the wedding, the father would place a veil over the bride as a final indication of his consent to the marriage. The groom would then arrive to fetch the bride, and bring her back to his home where, in a short ceremony, their marriage would be sealed. In this ceremony, the parents of the couple are seated before the family altar. The couple would then bow to heaven and earth, their ancestors, their parents, and each other. This is followed by the tea ceremony. This rite has been largely replaced by the solemnization of a marriage at the National Registrar of Marriages or in church, though some still carry out the traditional rites.

Biblical Approach: While the church acknowledges marriages solemnized at the National Registrar of Marriages as valid marital unions, it encourages all Christians to seal their commitment to their respective mates before God in a church. This, a) so their vows to each other may be witnessed by God and the whole body of Christ; b) serves as an invitation to God to be a vital binding thread in the union; and c) serves to seek the blessing and empowerment of God for the couple's new life together. Christians are cautioned against becoming superstitious in their adherence to certain cultural norms (for example, picking up the bride before the sun rises). In addition, we are not to engage in the solemnization ceremony before the family altar, due to its religious overtones.

The Tea Ceremony

For many today, the practical reason for holding a tea ceremony is the collection of *ang pows* (red packets)! This was not, however, the original purpose of the ceremony. Originally, the tea ceremony served two purposes. First, it was a sign of acceptance. By receiving tea from the bride, members of the bridegroom's family express their acceptance of the bride into the family. Should any member of the family, particularly the elders, refuse to accept the tea proffered, the bride would be in serious trouble! Thus, in earlier days, the tea ceremony served as a rite of initiation and acceptance into the family of the groom. Second, the tea ceremony was a time of formal introduction. This was particularly relevant in an age of arranged marriages, as the couple probably did not have much contact with each other till maybe a week or so before the wedding. The bride would not, therefore, know the family of the groom very well, if at all. During the tea ceremony, each family member is introduced to the bride, and along with this introduction is stated the family hierarchy and the place of the bride within this hierarchy. The mother-in-law would also take this opportunity to inform the bride of her duties in the family.

Biblical Approach: It can be quite redundant for one to hold such a tea ceremony today. While the acceptance of their marriage by family members remains important, many couples today are concerned only with the approval of their parents. In fact, even in ancient times, no marriage is usually held without the prior consent of the parents of the couple. In addition, most courting couples today would have met the family members of a prospective spouse long before the wedding. Generally speaking, in a society where weddings are often conducted at the National Registrar of Marriages or in a church, we do not really need the tea ceremony any more. Nonetheless, there is nothing really wrong with holding to it as a cultural practice that expresses our respect for our parents and our gratitude to them for bringing us up. Kneeling before our parents at such ceremonies is not considered an act of worship but a mark of respect. The concern rests with the practice of holding the tea ceremony before the ancestral altar, and the offering of tea to the ancestors to seek their approval and blessing.

Christians planning for a tea ceremony should seek to hold it in a place removed from the ancestral altar, so as not to get caught up in the practice of ancestral worship (where tea is poured out to the ancestors as an offering and to seek their blessing). One might, for example, hold the ceremony in a private room at a restaurant before the wedding dinner. Believers must, however, be prepared to make a stand against this practice (and primarily against the practice of ancestral worship), should all their attempts at holding the tea ceremony in a neutral environment fail.

Related Practices and Superstitions

The Matching of Horoscopes

It is a common practice for many parents to examine the horoscopes of the couple before agreeing to any match. Many matches have been objected to and broken, because the horoscopes of the couple are not deemed to be compatible.

Biblical Approach: Believers are to have nothing to do with this practice of divination. Our lives are in the hands of God and we have the personal responsibility to live well according to the Word of God, which teaches us to denounce and reject any involvement with such practices (Deuteronomy 18:10ff). Whatever our horoscopes might be, the real issue lies in submitting and committing our relationships to God.

The Dowry

In Chinese traditional practice, it is customary for the bridegroom to pay a certain dowry (also known as the bride price). In polite terms, this dowry is to thank and compensate the parents of the bride for having brought their daughter up. It is also to provide for the parents, as they now no longer have a daughter to live with and look after them. In ancient tradition, the payment of this bride price rendered the bride the property of the bridegroom. The rights and duty of the parents over the bride were then transferred to the bridegroom. This also meant that the bridegroom had sexual and procreative rights over the bride. While some in certain parts of the world may still hold to such a view, many in the more developed and westernized nations do not. A dowry may still change hands, but this is done more in keeping with cultural tradition and as a "final" blessing of the parents to the bride (both sets of parents would normally purchase jewellery for the bride).

Biblical Approach: Sex and procreation is a gift of God to be enjoyed within marriage, and it serves to bond a couple together emotionally as well as physically. It is not a right belonging to the parents or the husband that may be bartered or sold. A dowry — to thank and bless the parents of the bride, and as a traditional practice — may be given, but all parties concerned (the bride and groom and both sets of parents) should avoid making excessive requests.

An Alternative: It is good for couples to acknowledge the love and care of their parents. Some have sought to do this during their wedding dinners with the presentation of presents and bouquets, but this is not a regular feature of most marriage events. Should Christians and the church make the acknowledgement of parents a more regular and important feature of a marriage ceremony? I believe it is good that we do. In fact, I know of some churches that create space within the order of service for the happy couple to present gifts and say a few words of appreciation to their parents and in-laws.

The Timing of the Wedding

Many would seek to consult the Chinese almanac for an auspicious date for the wedding. In traditional practice, couples would get married before *Chun Jie* (Chinese New Year) and never during *Zhong Yuan Jie* (the Hungry Ghost Festival month). The former is desired because it is considered a great blessing to have an addition to the family before the New Year. The latter, because of all the roaming *kui* from hell that would be present everywhere.

Biblical Approach: Believers are not to hold to such beliefs. The sovereign Lord who watches over us to protect and provide is more than able to do so, regardless of the timing of our marriage. Nonetheless, grace may be shown to the cultural sensitivities of our non-Christian parents and relatives. For example, it is good for us not to hold weddings during *Zhong Yuan Jie*. For practical reasons, though, this could be the best time for Christians to do so as restaurants offer discounted rates because most Chinese would not want to hold major events in this inauspicious month. In opting not to hold a wedding celebration during this festival, we are not fearfully buying into the belief that the gates of hell are open. Rather, our desire is simply not to put our non-Christian relatives and friends in a dilemma with regard to whether or not they should attend our wedding.

With regard to the *Teochew* practice of specifying when a bride should leave her home, this is a pure superstition. Nonetheless, it is a fairly minor issue so believers may want to avoid arguing over this, especially if they have to make a firmer stand on other issues, like the performance of the tea ceremony before the ancestral altar and the offering of tea to their ancestors.

The Wedding Gown

The traditional Chinese wedding gown is called the *kua*. It is made of red material to symbolize blessings, and traditionally embroidered on it is the representation of the dragon and phoenix, symbolizing protection and life (longevity and fertility) respectively. In history, this was probably done on the wishes of the bride's parents as they sent her off to become a member of another family, that she might be protected on her journey and in her new home. It was also hoped that she might have a good long life and bear many children.

Biblical Approach: Ask people today what colour a wedding gown should be, and many would probably reply "white". Ask Christians if they may wear the *kua* and you would probably get a mixed response. The Bible does not specify what colours the bride and groom should wear on their wedding day. The use of the colour white is a Western import, arising from their cultural perception of white as symbolizing purity. To the Chinese, the colour symbolizes mourning and death, while red is the symbol of blessing. So, can believers walk down the church aisle in a red wedding gown? There is nothing in the Bible or church canon to stop it. It is simply a matter of personal preference.

What of the wearing of the *kua*? Does the church have any objections to it? In general, the answer is "no". The issue the church and most Christians have is not with the *kua* per se, but with what is traditionally embroidered on it, that is, the dragon and the phoenix (see Appendix A and Appendix E). These are held to be idolatrous images that believers should have nothing to do with. While we need not be afraid of these images, it is good for us, bearing in mind our Christian witness, to refrain from wearing anything with these symbols embroidered on them. It would not be good for us to tell those caught up in the veneration and worship of these symbols to remove them from their midst, and yet have the same symbols among our belongings.

An Alternative: The *kua* is a very beautiful cultural heritage to be preserved. In doing so, however, we should be careful about our Christian witness, that we do not cause our "weaker brethren" to stumble (1 Corinthians 8:9ff). Should we decide to wear the *kua*, let us choose one that is not embroidered with images of the dragon or phoenix. There are many other beautiful designs we can select.

The Warding Off of Ill Fortune

To ward off ill luck over the marriage, those from the *Hokkien* dialect group would tie sugar canes to the bridal car and doorpost of the home of the bridal couple. This practice dates back to an event that took place in the days of the *Song* dynasty (960-1279 AD). An emperor of this dynasty had become very angry with the *Hokkien* people for siding with a certain rebel group that was trying to overthrow the empire. In his wrath, the emperor ordered a massacre of the *Hokkien* people. Many were killed but some escaped by hiding themselves in sugar cane fields. Since then, the sugar cane has been for the *Hokkien* people a symbol of protection and blessing. Another common practice is for the bride to be sheltered with a red umbrella. The colour red is an auspicious colour for the Chinese, symbolizing joy and blessing. The use of an umbrella has to do with a play on the Mandarin word for umbrella, *yu shan*, particularly the word *shan*. This word sounds like the word used for "avoiding" or "warding off", that is, *shan kai*. The idea is that the red (auspicious) umbrella (*yu shan*), may ward off (*shan kai*) all evil.

Biblical Approach: If we do not delve too deeply into the superstitious connotations of the various practices — for example, tying sugar cane to the bridal car and sheltering the bride with a red umbrella — we may simply accept them as a way of communicating well wishes to the couple. The problem is that many do not just view these practices as symbolic, but actually believe that if they are not done, evil may well befall the bridal couple. Believers are not to propagate such superstitious practices and beliefs, and need not do so, as our sovereign Lord is more than able to protect us from evil and ill fortune (Job 1:10). In any case, few couples today would want to decorate their bridal cars with sugar cane or other similar ancient symbols of blessing and protection. Yet, should we be caught in a situation beyond our control — as when a red umbrella is produced without prior arrangement — we need not create a scene by saying, for example, that we would not get out of the car until the umbrella is removed.

The Desire for a Male Child

The desire for a male heir remains a top priority in many families, even for those who do not subscribe to the various Chinese religions. Take my late mother, for example, a Christian who before my son came along, had only two granddaughters. When my wife got pregnant, my mother helped with the preparations for the arrival of the child. As we did not perform a prenatal scan to find out the sex of the baby, my wife and I did not bother too much with the colour of the pillow and clothes for the child. After my wife had delivered a baby boy, one of my nieces innocently remarked, "Oh, it is a boy, Grandma will be most happy. She wants a boy as everything she has bought and made for the baby is blue in colour." My niece had innocently read my mother's heart desire.

For the Chinese, the birthing of a male child is an act of filial piety. This thought is connected to the Confucian concept of filial piety, which advocates the provision of an heir to continue the family name to be an act of filial piety.[4] For example, if I were the only or last male child of the family, with no male children of my own, the implication is that there will be no one to make offerings to me or my ancestors after I am dead and gone. Neither will there be anyone to carry on the family name to the next generation, which, to the Chinese, effectively means that the family no longer exists. As a result, I would have failed in my duty and be deemed not filial to my ancestors. This is why for centuries, right up to this very day, the Chinese have always wanted a male child, whose responsibility is to perpetuate the spread of the family name and see to the continued care of the family ancestral altar.

In times past, it was common to have a young boy jump up and down on the bed of the newly-wed, in the hope that this would result in the couple bearing a male child. Another practice was to place a cock and a hen under the marriage bed and wait to see which came out first. The belief was that should the cock be the first to emerge from under the bed, the first child of the couple would be male, and vice versa. In such a practice, woe to the bride should the hen be the first to emerge from under the bed.

Biblical Approach: Children are a gift of God (Genesis 20:17,18; 1 Samuel 2:21; Psalm 127:3) and it is He alone, our Creator, who determines their sex. Whether we receive a male or female child, we must recognise that all are a precious and perfect gift of God. Both male and female were created and given to each other by God for the sake of companionship and mutual support (Genesis 2:18ff). Christians are not, therefore, to hold any bias towards either sex, or engage in any means (superstitious or scientific) in pursuit of a child of any one particular sex. Neither are we to allow any concern with regard to the care of the ancestral altar or the continuance of the family name to cause us to desire and love a male child more than a female child.

General Evaluation

We need the wisdom of God to guide us concerning the acceptability of the various practices related to the marriage event. In general, grace is shown to certain cultural sensitivities (like not holding the event during *Zhong Yuan Jie* and not fussing over being sheltered by a red umbrella) and in these areas, we should simply accept things at their face value and not ask too many probing questions. A definite stand must, however, be taken against participation in any non-Christian rites and ancestral worship

(1 Corinthians 10:21), for example, the paying of obeisance to the family deity and offering of tea to the ancestors. Where we can avoid a confrontation, we should, but where we cannot, we must make a stand for our faith in Christ.

Ancestral Veneration

Chapter 6
Theological Perceptions

Contribution of Chinese Religious Beliefs

Ancestral worship is an integral part of Chinese religious practice. First practised in the *Hsia* dynasty, it underwent significant development in the *Chou* dynasty (1122-325 BC).[1] The Confucian teaching on filial piety, which advocates that parents and elders be respected while they are alive and continue to be revered when dead, has helped popularize ancestral worship. In discussing ancestral veneration and worship, we deal with that which is most commonly practised in traditional Chinese families today.[2] To begin, it is important for us to understand the main tenets and rites of this practice, which is a combination of Confucianism, Buddhism, Daoism and Shenism (local folk religions and animistic practices).

Influence of Confucianism

The contribution of Confucianism to the practice of ancestral worship is the concept of filial piety, which advocates that each individual has both a physical and a spiritual obligation to fulfil towards his elders. The former refers to our catering to the bodily needs of our parents, care for our own bodies as a legacy from our ancestors, and the rearing of children to provide for the continuity of our family. The latter includes obedience to our parents (even after their death), remembrance of our deceased ancestors with annual sacrifices, and the gaining of success and honour to bring glory to the family name. These obligations serve as a bridge between the practical duties of this world and the religious concern for life after death. In Confucianism, the family unit is considered to be more important than the individual. This does not mean that the individual is not important, but just that when a choice between the two has to be made — welfare of the family versus the need of the individual — the family (corporate unit) takes precedence. The five duties filial children are to perform (see Figure 5: Confucian and Biblical Concepts of Filial Piety) teach us to care for our elders while they are alive, and even after they are dead.

Confucius also advocated a belief in *Tien Ming*, the Mandate of Heaven, which holds that in all things, heaven knows best and will take care of everything. A problem with this belief is that the will of heaven is discerned according to whether or not one prospers in his endeavour/s. What happens if a person prospers despite being underhanded and wicked, or despite being a murderer and thief? Is he in the will of heaven? Confucianism calls upon us to continue to believe in and seek the will and guidance of our ancestors, even after their death. The will of our ancestors is deemed to be equivalent to the mandate of heaven that must be obeyed without question. In practical terms, this means that my children have to obey every rule and regulation that I, as head of the house, lay down. Even after my death, my children, grandchildren and great-grandchildren would have to continue to keep these rules and regulations.

You may wonder what we are to do should we have a wicked person or criminal for an ancestor or parent. Well, Confucian ethic also teaches that one is to resist when wrongly commanded (see Figure 5). This means that we can say "no" to our elders should we be commanded to do something that is wrong. For example, if I am a thief and murderer, the rules and regulations I lay down for my family would, in all likelihood, reflect my lifestyle. Is my family then to follow in my footsteps? In Confucianism, the

Figure 5: Confucian and Biblical Concepts of Filial Piety

Confucian Concept Of Filial Piety	**Honour Your Parents (Exodus 20:12)**
1. The family unit is more important than the individual. 2. The will of our ancestors is equated to the Mandate of Heaven that must be obeyed without question. 3. Five duties to perform • Venerate parents in daily life • Ensure their happiness • Take extra care of them when they fall sick • Show great sorrow at their death • Offer sacrifices to the deceased parents. 4. Provide an heir to continue the family name. 5. Resist when wrongly commanded.	1. We are to provide and care for our parents. (Mark 7:9-13) 2. We are to obey our parents. (Ephesians 6:1,4) 3. We are not to rebuke our parents sharply. (1 Timothy 5:1,2) 4. We are not to curse or speak ill of our parents. (Exodus 21:17; Mark 7:10b)

answer is "no". My family should, instead, learn from the wise ethical teachings of others, resisting my evil lifestyle.

Many who engage in ancestral worship have interpreted Confucius' teaching on the primacy of ancestral wisdom to mean that we may communicate with our deceased ancestors. For example, a few years ago, there was an article about the residents of a village in Japan whose first act upon reaching home was to appear before the ancestral altar to commune with their departed, whom they believe would literally communicate with them. Addressing this phenomenon, Dr *Hidehiko Jose* notes, "The dead counsel the living. Talking with the dead is widespread, and maybe that's the reason why mental health care has lagged so much in Japan."[3] It is not right for us to interpret the teaching of Confucius in this way.

Biblical Approach: Taking note of the commandment to honour our father and mother (Exodus 20:12) and care for them (Matthew 15:1-9), Christians need have no problem accepting the physical obligations stated. Achieving success and honour for the family is quite acceptable, so long as no underhanded means are applied (for example, extortion, theft and cheating). We must, however, examine closely the stipulated spiritual obligations. Of concern is the injunction to continue to make offerings to and care for our parents even after their death. The Bible does not teach that this may be done, or even if it can be done, that it would result in any real blessings befalling our dearly departed in the afterlife. The offering of sacrifices must not be practised, due to its connotation as an act of worship. While they are to be remembered, our ancestors are not to be worshipped. Worship is reserved for our Lord and Saviour Jesus Christ alone. In addition, the time to show filial piety is while our parents are still alive, not after they are dead and gone (Hebrews 9:27).

Do Christians believe in the concept of *Tien Ming*? No, we do not. We do, however, believe in a sovereign Creator who is actively engaged in our lives. He reveals His will to us through His Word, and other believers, for example. He blesses us with abundance and provides for all our material needs (Matthew 6:25-34), teaching us to cherish, but not get caught up with, the material things of this world (1 Timothy 6:7-12). He condemns thievery, murder and wickedness as sin, at times saving His children from having to suffer these, yet at others simply strengthening them physically, emotionally and spiritually to go through trials (Acts 12). In all circumstances, our Lord God is sovereignly in charge to work things out for the good of those who love and put their trust in Him (Romans 8:28).

As Christians, we are to obey our parents (Ephesians 6:1-3). Regardless of the situation, we are not to sharply rebuke them (1 Timothy 5:1,2), or curse or speak ill of them (Exodus 21:17; Mark 7:10b). For the Chinese, obedience to the deceased often means communicating with the dead to seek instruction, or following the lessons taught during the lifetime of the deceased. The Bible does not teach that the former should be done (Leviticus 19:31; Deuteronomy 18:10-12) but the latter is quite acceptable (provided the teaching does not contravene the Word of God). For believers, the will of our elders is not equivalent to the mandate of heaven. We honour our parents by obeying them, but our ultimate authority is the Bible (2 Timothy 3:16).

An Alternative: While alive, our parents should be respected, honoured and obeyed (Exodus 20:12). All the knowledge and wisdom of our ancestors, passed down through the ages, should be remembered and used to guide us in our lives. All traditions, regardless of their origin and what they teach, must be checked against the Bible to ensure that they are consistent with and advocate the will of our Lord Jesus Christ.

Influence of Buddhism

The introduction of Buddhism into China led to the assimilation of the concepts of reincarnation, and the accumulation and transference of merit, into the practice of ancestral veneration. These notions are in line with the Buddhist belief that salvation is attained through self-effort, self-emancipation and self-conquest.[4] The belief is held that we will be reborn over and over again into this world until we attain enlightenment. This means that we, and our ancestors, have a second (or more) chance after our deaths to try to attain enlightenment. In addition, to aid us in getting reincarnated, certain rites and duties have to be performed, like meditating on and chanting the *sutra*.[5] These duties need not necessarily be done by the person seeking enlightenment but may be carried out in proxy by his descendants. So, with the passing of a loved one, those who are still living may meditate or engage monks to recite the *sutras* for the deceased to help them accumulate the necessary merits.

Biblical Approach: The purpose of reincarnation is the progressive purification or evolutionary development of an individual. The belief in reincarnation is a very human-centred approach towards seeking salvation. It lacks the backing of the Bible and is incompatible with a number of central beliefs within the Christian faith, for example, the resurrection of the body, and salvation not by works but by grace through faith in Christ (Ephesians 2:8). The Bible teaches that when we die, we end up either in the bosom of Abraham / Paradise or *Hades* / *Sheol* (Luke 16:22; 23:43). We do not know where these places are, but we shall remain there without any contact with those yet alive or the possibility of reincarnation, to await the return of our Lord Jesus Christ.

An Alternative: The sacrifice of our Lord Jesus Christ on the cross at Calvary secures salvation for everyone who believes in and accepts Him as Lord and Saviour (John 3:16). The ultimate price has been paid for all our sins, and we have been wholly and freely redeemed. We need not, therefore, seek any form of merit in order to earn our way to heaven. We would not be able to accumulate enough merit in any case, even if we tried.

Influence of Daoism

In Daoism, the death of an individual represents a disruption of the balance within the cosmos, which may be re-established only through the performance of certain (death) rituals by the Daoist priests. The *Dao Jiao* school of Daoism believes that we may achieve immortality through the performance of certain rites and rituals that would bring us into harmony with the universal *Dao*. Daoism brings into ancestral worship the idea that the performance of certain rites may lead the dead out of hell and into heaven to become an immortal or deity. Hence, at many Chinese funerals, there are rituals that require the family to walk around the coffin, etc.

Biblical Approach: The performance of rites and rituals again constitutes a vain human attempt to attain salvation by personal effort. The Bible is clear that the only way for us to gain salvation is to make a decision today, while we are yet alive, to confess all our sins before God and receive Jesus Christ into our hearts as Lord and Saviour (John 3:18-21). The Bible does not teach a belief in the *Dao*, but a belief that all things are the creation of God (Genesis 1). No belief is to be placed in the efficacy of rituals. None but God is sovereign over the whole of creation, life and death, and no rites can influence His decisions and His ways.

Influence of Shenism

Shenism imputes a more mystical and superstitious character to the practice of ancestral worship. Chinese tribal folk religion presents ancestral worship with a belief in a pantheon of deities and a concept of what the spirit world and afterlife may be like. It presents the idea that there is a spirit world parallel to our physical realm to which our dearly departed go when they die. In this spirit world, a pantheon of spirits and deities rule, functioning in ways similar to how we in the physical realm would function (for example, the need for food and clothing, and the hierarchical court system). These spirits (both *shen* and *kui*) are believed to be those of our dearly departed.

Biblical Approach: While the Bible does speak of spirits, it identifies them as demons and evil spirits (1 Chronicles 16:26; Psalm 96:5), not our dearly departed transformed into *shen* or *kui*. Believers are not to be deceived by the demons behind this belief (1 Corinthians 10:20).

Belief in the Afterlife

The Chinese believe that the involvement of an individual in the lives and affairs of his family does not end with death, which is viewed as a mere transition. Ancestors are seen to provide economic, emotional and social security for the family; this helps the family view itself not as an individual unit, but as part of a long continuum of descent. The continued relationship and inter-dependence between the living and the dead reinforce the family as a social unit.

The *Yin* World

The Chinese hold to a belief in the Western Paradise and the *Yin* World in the afterlife. The former refers to the abode of deities and immortals, while the latter to the place where the dead are judged. The spirit world is believed to be a mirror image of the human world, anthropomorphic in nature in the sense that those in it experience the same appetites (lust, greed and hunger), customs (marriage), needs (housing and money) and desires (the search for immortality) as those in the physical human realm. A filial child would ensure the provision of "material possessions" for the comfort of the departed in the spirit world.

Biblical Approach: The Bible teaches of a new heaven and a new earth to come, where there shall be no tears, suffering or sorrow (Revelation 21:1,2,4). A belief in the Chinese concept of the spirit world with its anthropomorphic nature finds no support in the Bible. Though the Bible gives a brief description of the New Jerusalem,[6] there is no clear account of the lifestyle and manner in which we are to live, apart from the fact that we shall spend our time serving and worshipping God (Revelation 19:1-7). The Bible is also silent on the exact nature of the intermediate state (that time and place between death and resurrection while one awaits the return of Christ). It does imply, however, that no human aid is necessary as all that we need would be more than adequately supplied by our Lord God (Deuteronomy 8:1-4; Psalm 139:7-10). In the Bible a distinction is made between the abode of believers (in Christ) and non-believers upon their demise. The former is pictured to be safe in the bosom of Abraham (Luke 16:22) while the latter is shown to be in *Hades* (Luke 16:22,23). However, apart from the connotation of fiery torment attached to *Hades* , the Bible gives no other description of either of these "places".

An Alternative: References to *Sheol* may be found in the Old Testament (Job 7:9; Isaiah 38:10), while references to *Hades* are made in the New Testament (Matthew 11:23; Luke 16:23). These terms generally refer to the same place, which the Bible points to as that place where the deceased reside while awaiting the return of Christ.[7] The Bible does not, however, elaborate on either its location or composition. With the return of Christ, all will be judged and sent to their final eternal abode. Those who believe in and have turned to Christ will enter into the presence of God, their ultimate destination being a transformed universe, "a new heaven and a new earth" (Revelation 21:1-7). Unbelievers will be thrown into "the lake that burns with fire and brimstone" (Revelation 21:8), which symbolizes the utter destruction of those excluded from the presence of God.

Judgement, Merit and Reincarnation

Out of the Buddhist and Daoist religions grew the concept of the 10 halls of judgement (see Appendix D), consisting of 18 levels of punishment. The Chinese believe there is a deity over every town and city that records all our good and evil deeds. Upon our death, this deity will send the Ox-head and Horse-face spirits to bring our souls down to the first court of hell. It is believed that the Book of Death and Life is kept in this court. After a person dies, this is his first stop, where the Book is opened to reveal how he has lived his life. From this stop, he is sent to the different courts for judgement, depending on the merit gained.[8] After he has passed through all 10 halls, the Buddhist concept of reincarnation comes into play. If a person has lived a good life, he is sent directly to the tenth court for the final judgement. This court will determine the form in which the deceased will be reincarnated, be it as a beast, human or insect.

Where and how we end up at death, is determined by the amount of merit we have accumulated, whether through meditation (of the Buddhist *sutras*) or good works. The merit helps us to avoid punishment, pass quickly through the halls and be reincarnated. Deliverance may also be achieved through the performance of certain Daoist rites and for some, bribery. The latter belief arises from the view that the spirit world parallels the human world in its lifestyle. For some, this means that just as people in the human world can be bribed, so can the guards and court officials of the spirit world. This encourages people to burn as much "hell money" as they can possibly afford to their loved ones in hell. A person will continue to return to the *Yin* World upon the death of each reincarnation, till enough merit has been accumulated for the soul to proceed to the Western Paradise.

Biblical Approach: The Bible teaches that all have sinned and deserve to be judged and punished (Romans 3:23). None may accumulate, through any self-effort, the merit needed to attain salvation. Jesus Christ, however, has died for our sins and won for us the ultimate merit (John 3:16-18). As a whole, the concept of reincarnation is contrary to the Christian faith because its basic premise is the attainment of rebirth into a superior form through self-effort. The Bible states that God has created each of us with a specific lifespan (Job 7:1; Psalm 90:10), and that at death, we will "go the way of no return" (Job 16:22). The Bible is also crystal clear in its teaching that Jesus is the way, the truth and the life, and none may come to God the Father but through Him (John 14:6).

Concept of the Soul

The Chinese have a very interesting concept of the soul. They believe that each person has three souls.[9] This belief may strike a chord with Christians, as the Bible does, at times, refer to human beings as body, soul and spirit (1 Thessalonians 5:23); we will delve into this in the section below. The Chinese believe that upon the death of a person, the souls are dispersed to reside in three different places. One soul departs from this world to receive judgement or reward in the *Yin* World or Western Paradise, respectively. Another soul resides in the ancestral tablet. The common practice is for rites to be performed on the forty-ninth day after a person has passed away to invite the soul of the deceased to enter and reside in the ancestral tablet. The third soul is said to reside in the body of the deceased; this has resulted in the Chinese myth that a corpse may well rise up and become a vampire. Practitioners of Daoism and *feng shui* (the Chinese practice of geomancy) draw from the belief that a soul resides in the body of the deceased, to advocate the importance of siting the tomb in the right manner and place.

Biblical Approach: How many souls are there — one, two or three? In Christianity, answers have been given depending largely on whether one belongs to the Western church or subscribes to Eastern Orthodox traditions. Christianity in the West commonly maintains a tripartite view (body, soul and spirit — 1 Thessalonians 5:23) of the nature of man, whereas Eastern Orthodoxy would often speak of the body and soul or body and spirit (Matthew 10:28; 1 Corinthians 5:3).[10] The Bible does not separate an individual into two or more parts, nor does it give a detailed description of the composition and make-up of human beings. In the Bible, the word "soul" is often used interchangeably with the word "spirit". God looks upon and deals with us as a whole. For example, in redemption, our Lord does not merely redeem the spirit (as a result of the view that the body is evil and corrupt). He redeems the whole person; body, soul and spirit. The Chinese concept of the three souls and their abode upon the death of a person, finds no basis and support in the Bible. Christians are not, therefore, to believe in this teaching. The Bible is clear that after death, a person is interred either in *Hades* or the bosom of Abraham (Luke 16:22f) to await the return of our Lord Jesus Christ on the Last Day.[11]

Shen and *Kui*

Have you ever asked yourself who the hungry ghosts are and where they come from? If truth be told, in Chinese belief, they are actually our ancestors. How can this be, you may well ask. The belief goes that after a person dies he becomes a spirit being. If he has accumulated enough merit while alive or is well taken care of — through rites performed and prayers said on his behalf, and the "hell money", luxuries and food burnt as offerings to him — by his descendants, he will go to heaven and become a *shen* (deity or immortal).

On the other hand, should the deceased have led an evil life and is not cared for (with rites and offerings) after death, he would become a *kui* (a wandering ghost or evil spirit) of hell. With no offerings of "hell money" or food, the *kui* becomes a wandering ghost and a hungry one to boot. During *Zhong Yuan Jie*, offerings are laid out for these hungry ghosts, both out of compassion for their plight and for protection from them.

Biblical Approach: The Bible teaches that no one may accumulate merit to be used to attain entrance into heaven. It maintains that salvation is given to us purely by the grace and mercy of God (Romans 3:24,28), and may be appropriated only by faith (Galatians 2:16). It also does not teach any belief in the gates of hell being thrown open once a year for the *kui* to roam the earth in search of food and entertainment. There is no biblical basis for a belief in the Chinese concepts of *shen* and *kui*. All, upon death, are consigned to *Hades* or the bosom of Abraham (Luke 16:22ff), and may not depart from these places at any time except on the last day to stand before the judgement seat of God.

A Related Superstition

One strand of Chinese belief holds that within a person, there are the *hun* (soul) and the *p'o* (life force).[12] The latter is thought to be in possession of an individual before his birth. At death, the *hun* leaves the body from an orifice in the cranium, while the *p'o* remains behind. Should the energy of the *p'o* be very strong, the corpse will possess great power and rise to commit terrible atrocities. It is also believed that the corpse may awaken and become a zombie should a black cat jump over it. If the body of the deceased is properly taken care of, however, the *p'o* will rest peacefully and the *hun* will pour forth blessings upon the surviving family members.[13]

Biblical Approach: The Chinese do not have a clearly formulated concept of the soul, for example, some advocate that there are two parts to each individual (see paragraph above), while others believe there are three. The Bible does not encourage a belief in this concept (see discussion on the Concept of the Soul). As Christians, we also do not believe in the superstition that a corpse may come back to life as a zombie to haunt us. The resurrection taught in the Bible occurs on the Last Day when our Lord Jesus returns and the dead are raised to stand before the judgement seat of God (Revelation 20:11-13).

An Alternative: The sense of fear generated by this superstition often binds people to the continued practice of ancestral veneration / worship. Believers need not be bound by this fear, as the love and sacrifice of our Lord Jesus Christ, along with our reciprocal love and acceptance of Him as our Lord and Saviour, cast out all fear (1 John 4:18,19).

Worship God Alone

In Chinese religious belief and practice, it is very difficult to draw a line between ancestral veneration and ancestral worship. For one, the Chinese perceive their ancestors to be spirits (*shen* or *kui*) who continue to be actively involved in the affairs of the physical human realm. No divide separates the living from the dead. For another, many practices associated with the care of ancestors are observed in the worship of Chinese deities and gods (such as the manner in which prayers are said and offerings made).

In Christianity, a clear distinction is made between God, humanity and demonic spirits. In addition, clear divides separate the living from the dead, and the dead from evil demonic spirits (see Appendix C). Christianity makes a clear distinction between the worship of God and the worship of ancestors and various deities, and teaches that worship is to be directed towards God alone. As Christians, we respect our ancestors but we do not worship them as deities. We remember our dearly departed and give thanks for the wisdom passed down to us, but we do not seek to communicate with the deceased or have them influence our lives.

Tradition and Practicality

Centred on the ancestral tablet, funeral and grave, ancestral worship today is practised for three basic reasons: a child's respect for his parents (a central virtue in Chinese teachings); the belief that the deceased continue to live with their living offspring; and a belief in the ability of the deceased to either bless or curse the living.[14] More often than not, the practice of ancestral veneration is not formally taught or enforced. Rather, it is the result of observing and unconsciously assimilating into our own lives, the acts of worship performed by those who are dear and close to us. The Chinese generally hold to a traditional worldview, and their ethic for living is set by the community, not the individual. This helps us to understand the acceptance and continued practice of ancestral veneration in Chinese society.

From Generation to Generation

Ancestral veneration (and the form it takes among different people) is a practice handed down from one generation to the next. This tradition is continued by the younger generations either out of a genuine belief in it and its underlying tenets, or at the insistence of their elders who fear for their afterlife existence if none are around to make offerings to them. Many keep this practice out of respect for their elders (filial piety), and as a result of habits or worship patterns established since early childhood.

Biblical Approach: The attempt to retain certain aspects of our Asian and family heritage is praiseworthy. Nevertheless, we need to check these traditions and heritages against the Bible, to ensure that they do not contravene the commands and will of God. Habits and worship patterns carried over from our past as non-believers must be examined in the light of the Word of God, and those which are against the teachings of the Word must be discarded. The concern of our elders over how they would live and the offerings they would receive after their death is very much linked to their understanding of the afterlife. Believers do not hold to the same concerns because the sacrifice and finished work of our Lord Jesus Christ on the cross ensure our salvation (John 3:16-18), spiritual heritage (Galatians 4:7), and a place in the kingdom of God where sorrow shall cease (Revelation 21:4).

An Alternative: The handing down of beliefs and values from one generation to another is a common and most effective means of character development, the potential of which Christians should learn to tap. We must, however, ensure that the beliefs and values we communicate are based on the Word of God. Parents and elders must, therefore, work at living a Christ-centred and Christ-like life, worthy for our offspring to emulate.

For Personal Gain and Blessing

Self-interest is another reason to engage in ancestral worship. Here, an individual may be seeking personal gratification; offerings are made in the hope of pleasing the spirit of the deceased to gain favour and blessing. Alternatively, the individual could well desire to please or pacify the *shen* or *kui* out of fear being harmed.

Biblical Approach: Our Lord Jesus Christ is Lord over all, and as His children we need not fear the attacks of any spirit (Luke 10:18-20). As for personal gain and self-interest, we need to acknowledge that our Lord knows and provides for all our needs (Psalm 147:7-9). In addition, we must learn to die to ourselves daily, being well aware of the danger of succumbing to the temptations of lust and greed (Matthew 16:24-28).

Chapter 7
Practical Considerations

The Funeral Rite

The funeral rite deals with the encoffining of one of the three souls that the Chinese believe a person has, and assisting of the second soul on its trip to the Western Paradise.

The Encoffining

Before the encoffining, the deceased is ceremonially washed, so that the spirits of the *Yin* World might not be offended by the appearance. Personal items are often placed in the coffin, for use in the afterlife. In the past, coffins were made in the shape of a house, because of the belief that one of the souls of the deceased resides in the tomb. It was also common for one of the following items to be placed in the mouth of the deceased: a coin, with which to bribe the officials of the *Yin* World; some grains of rice, to ensure the dead never grow hungry; or a pearl to light the way for the deceased in the underworld.

Biblical Approach: Believers do not believe in the practice of ceremonially washing the body (the normal procedures of embalming the deceased would suffice) or the inclusion of personal items for use in the afterlife, as we hold no belief in the anthropomorphic *Yin* World or the spirits therein. Personal items may, however, be placed in the coffin, not for use in the afterlife, but as a remembrance of the personal possessions that the departed treasured and liked. Clear teaching must be given (through the generations) to ensure that this act of remembrance does not take on the features of a Chinese religious belief in an anthropomorphic afterlife. There is also no need to make the coffin in the shape of a house, as the Bible does not speak of us residing in the tomb after our death.

The Funeral Wake

It is normal for the body to be laid out for a few days (normally in the odd numbers of three, five and seven days, which have some superstitious reference to good and bad luck) to allow friends and relatives to pay their last respects. The longer the period of mourning, the more respect and love the family members are showing to their dearly departed. In ancient times, the period of mourning that followed the burial of the deceased would last for 100 days, following which no one in the family was to get married over the next one to three years. For some, the length of this period of mourning is used to gauge the popularity of the deceased among family members and friends. Long mourning periods are not common these days, and though people still keep to the rule of having the wake over an odd number of days, practical considerations are normally the deciding factor for its length. One of these factors is the time it would take for all relatives and friends to attend the wake and pay their last respects.

Another gauge of the popularity of the deceased is the amount and volume of crying that occurs at a wake. To the Chinese, if no one cries at a funeral, it either means that the family is not filial to the deceased, or that the deceased was not a nice person and was thus not missed by anyone. To avoid such gossip, people in the past hired professional mourners to cry at the funerals of their dearly departed. At the wake, the immediate family members would kneel to the side of the altar behind which the body of the deceased is laid. Visitors who come to pay their last respects would first stand before the altar and bow, offer some incense, and then turn to bow to the kneeling family members.

Biblical Approach: It is good for the body to be laid out for a few days to allow friends and relatives to pay their last respects and say their final farewells. This aids the grieving process, whereby all are given the opportunity to mourn and come to terms with the loss. This practice also serves to show that our departed is not quickly and easily forgotten, which is an important witness to non-believers. As to the hiring of professional mourners, it is interesting to note that there is mention of such a practice in Amos 5:16. This is not licence, however, for Christians to engage in this practice. The Bible does not teach us to wail loudly in mourning; it advocates that we are to show filial piety while our elders are alive, with no necessity to proclaim it publicly after they are dead. Besides, if our dearly departed was a Christian, we are assured that though he is absent from us on earth, we will meet again in heaven (1 Thessalonians 4:16-18).

On the issue of bowing, it is important for us to determine the manner and context within which it is done. For example, when accepting my degree upon graduation, I bowed to the person presenting the certificate and to the congregation. What was I doing? Was I expressing worship? No, I was not. In this context, the bows simply express my thanks and respect. When standing before the coffin of the deceased, the context changes, and so does the meaning of our bows. For some Chinese Christians, bowing thus connotes the paying of our last respects and is acceptable so long as we are not holding any joss sticks in our hands. Bowing before an altar with joss sticks in hand carries a different connotation — one of worship — and is discouraged. At the wake, believers should politely refuse if offered joss sticks to place before the deceased. Most people would not insist on a visitor having to do so. It is sufficient for believers to simply stand beside the coffin and view the body, offering a short prayer for the surviving members of the family.

An Alternative: A Christian wake can serve as a witness to non-believers in its quiet simplicity, which expresses the assurance of our victory over death (1 Corinthians 15:12ff). Despite grieving over a loss, Christians can rejoice in the hope of seeing their loved ones again when our Lord Jesus Christ returns. In addition, memorial services may be held during some or all nights of the funeral wake. The purpose of this service is to a) minister to the living; b) allow for a show of support to the family of the deceased, by sharing in their loss; c) give both family and friends a time to remember, mourn and come to terms with the loss; and d) share the hope that all who believe in Christ are assured of a place and will be reunited in heaven.

Prayer for the Dead

Traditionally, on the final night of mourning, Daoist priests[15] are invited to perform various rites and rituals. This is done primarily to assist the deceased to escape from hell, and either get reincarnated into a better life or enter the Western Paradise. In Daoist rituals, family members, led by the eldest male child of the deceased carrying a lantern, would have to circle the coffin 10 times. The number of times the family goes around the coffin is determined by the prevailing belief in the number of levels of punishment in hell. The belief is that each time the family completes a circle of the coffin, the deceased is led up one level of hell and closer to an escape from it. The lantern carried by the male member of the family leading the procession is meant to light the way for the deceased. This process continues till the deceased has been led across a paper bridge, signifying the link between the *Yin* World and the Western Paradise. At this point, the leader of the procession must cry out loud to prompt the deceased to cross the bridge. The paper bridge is then burnt so the deceased may not accidentally wander back into hell, and to stop Ox-head and Horse-face, the guardian spirits of the *Yin* World, from crossing over to pursue the deceased.

Biblical Approach: No human being has the power and authority to save, let alone lead anyone out of hell. No rite performed by man can save (Ephesians 2:8,9). Only the Son of God, Jesus Christ, is able to save, having defeated death (1 Corinthians 15:55-58), and having in His possession the keys of hell (Revelation 1:17,18). The time to confess our sins and receive Christ into our hearts is now, while we are still alive, for we will get no second chance in death. Christians find no power or efficacy in Daoist rituals, and are instructed by the Bible to have nothing to do with them (1 Corinthians 10:21). To avoid participation in the rites to lead the deceased out of the *Yin* World, believers should make themselves known to the priests called upon to perform them as soon as they arrive at a wake. The priests would, more often than not, excuse believers from participating in these rites. In this regard, believers must not compromise, but take a stand.

It is almost unavoidable that converts, whose families are actively engaged in ancestral worship, would be confronted with the call to participate in funeral rites. A refusal to do so would undoubtedly earn us the tag of lacking in filial piety, but that really cannot be helped. What we must do is show filial piety in other non-religious or non-idolatrous ways. There are many things we can do for our parents without getting involved in the religious and superstitious, and compromising our faith in Jesus Christ, for example, doing the household chores, or cleaning and cooking for the family. As Christians, we are to honour our parents, first of all, as an act of obedience to the teachings of God recorded in the Bible (Exodus 20:12; Mark 7:9-13). Next, out of love for and gratitude towards our parents. Last, but not least, to discredit any who might try to accuse us of not being filial. To help avoid unpleasant confrontations and a wrenching of conscience (when we refuse our elders), it is important for converts to inform their immediate family of their new-found faith as soon as possible. Establish early the Christian standard of living without compromise, for example, no holding of joss sticks or burning of "hell money".

In Singapore, it is fairly common knowledge that believers will not participate in traditional Chinese funeral rites. This was brought very clearly to my attention a few years ago while I was helping a friend prepare for the funeral of one of his parents. In speaking to the funeral director of the casket company, which was a typical Chinese set-up, I noted that one of the first things he did was to have all the Christians in the family identify themselves. When that had been done, he went on, quite matter-of-factly, to say that these family members should simply stand aside and not participate in the funeral rites. Let us, therefore, not be afraid to identify ourselves as believers, particularly to the presiding Buddhist monk or Daoist priest. True practitioners of Buddhism and Daoism would not, generally, want believers to be present during their rites and rituals.

An Alternative: Prayers for the Lord to strengthen and comfort surviving family members may be said at wakes and funeral services. The services held should minister to the living, and serve as a time of remembrance. Should the deceased be a Christian, the salvation of that person in Christ should be reiterated, so family members may be comforted.

Burial of the Dead

As one soul is believed to reside in the tomb, the care of the tomb is very important. In traditional Chinese practice, the tomb is meant to facilitate the channelling and absorbing of *Da Qi* (vital breath or great vitality — the energy that animates the universe) by the corpse. It is thought that the absorbing of *Da Qi* helps preserve the corpse, allowing the deceased to "live on". The traditional Chinese domed tomb has been shaped according to Daoist principles of science and magic, which declare that the greatest concentration of *Da Qi* is found at the point where heaven and earth meet. As such, Chinese tombs represent the heavens, while the ground upon which they are sited represent the earth (see Figure 6: Shaping of a Traditional Chinese Tomb). *Feng shui* practitioners (those versed in reading the flow of the mystical life force of the universe) then step in to help families find the place and point of greatest concentration of *Da Qi*, and site the tomb in the best possible location and position.[16] Incorporated into the practice of ancestral worship is the belief that in blessing the corpse of the departed in such a way, the surviving descendants will be blessed in return, as the departed watches over them.[17]

Figure 6: Shaping of a Traditional Chinese Tomb

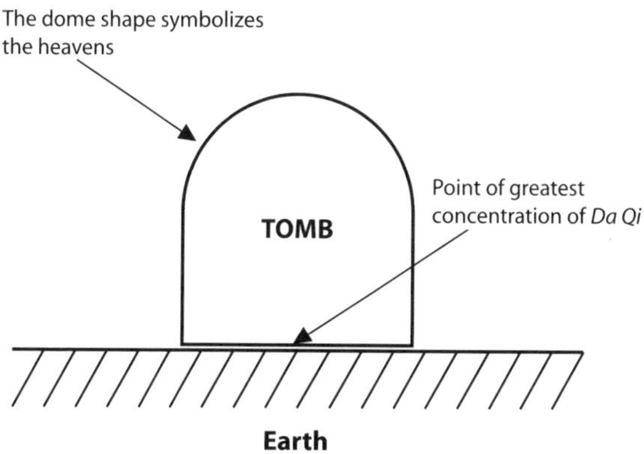

Biblical Approach: Christianity does not hold to or encourage a belief in *Da Qi*. The Bible does not teach that at death, one of our souls resides in the tomb, which, if properly built and sited, would bring great blessing to later generations. Neither the *feng shui* master who sites the tomb, nor the shape of the tomb, nor a belief in *Da Qi* can do anything for the deceased and his descendants. Jesus is the only one who can save us from our sins (John 3:16-21) and watches over us in this life on earth as we await His return. Christians are not to follow this practice, as it does not focus our attention on God, but on the self and self-effort, as well as a mystical force that does not stem from God.

Mourning Clothes

Traditionally, family members would dress in mourning clothes made of sackcloth for the funeral. In addition, the relationship between the mourner and the deceased is revealed by the colour of the clothes. White — a colour expressing deepest mourning — is worn by the spouse, sons and daughters, blue by grandchildren, green by great-grandchildren and black by close relatives (cousins and siblings). While some people today still wear these different colours, more and more are doing without them, preferring instead to dress simply in either black or white, with a patch of cloth on the sleeve to signify their relationship with the deceased.

Biblical Approach: In the Bible, dressing in sackcloth and the pouring of ashes over oneself expressed the deep sorrow, mourning and repentance of a person (Esther 4:1; Matthew 11:21). There does not appear to be any other motive apart from that of mourning too within the Chinese practice. There is, therefore, nothing wrong with Christians wearing sackcloth. As the Bible does not forbid or condemn the wearing of these garments, this issue is left to our individual conscience, taking into account the fact that the garments may be a means for believers to maintain a certain identity and solidarity with their families and their Chinese roots. Christians need have no objection to the wearing of cloth patches, but should refrain from the superstitious practice of requiring them to be burnt at the end of the funeral out of the belief that everything connected with the funeral must be set alight to avoid ill fortune.

Related Superstitions

There are various superstitions related to the funeral. For example, a band must lead the cortege to ward off evil spirits, and upon their return from the cemetery or crematorium, family members must wash their hands and faces, or cross over a small fire before entering the home, to signify the washing away of bad luck associated with the loss. This practice stems from the belief that spirits cannot pass through water and fire. Superstitious connotations may also be found in the items laid out for those who turn up to pay their respects to the deceased. For example, sweets are served to remove the bitterness (bitter taste in the mouth) of the loss. It is also common for a red thread to be given to those who have come to pay their respects to ensure their safe passage home.

These practices stem from the view that a funeral is a negative and sad event full of ill fortune. When well-wishers visit out of love and care for the family, it is not right to send them away with the possibility that they too may "inherit" this ill fortune. Red threads (and, at times, red packets with a coin inside) are thus given to help them ward off the bad fortune and evil associated with death. The more superstitious would, immediately upon leaving the funeral, burn the red thread or red packet to ensure that the ill fortune is totally gone and unable to "follow" them home.

Biblical Approach: Christians should not be concerned or fearful over the thought that ill fortune or evil is present at funerals and may trail us home, for our victory in Christ is absolute (1 Corinthians 15:56,57). In addition, our trust is in *Jehovah Jireh,* our Provider (Psalm 34; Proverbs 3:5,6) who knows our every need and will more than adequately and abundantly provide for them. Superstitious practices should not be followed for these reasons, and as a witness of our freedom from any bondage to fear (Isaiah 41:10; Matthew 10:26). It is okay for us to eat the sweets, groundnuts and melon seeds offered at wakes, as many today do not know their superstitious significance.[18] Christians, however, should avoid taking or giving out the red thread and packets — their superstitious meaning is fairly well understood — as a witness to non-believers that our God is Lord of the universe and far greater than any evil which seeks to harm us.

The Family Altar

In homes where ancestral worship is practised, a room or corner of the house is often set aside for the family altar. On this altar are placed the ancestral tablet/s (usually of immediate relations such as parents and grandparents; the tablets of earlier ancestors are usually put in the temple), the incense urn and two candles. Some food or fruit may also be left on the altar. A photograph of the deceased, however, is not to be found on the altar. Daily offerings of incense are laid on this altar, with special offerings and prayers made on the first and fifteenth of the month, and the death anniversary of the deceased.

Biblical Approach: Such an altar should not be found in a Christian home. Apart from serving as a bad witness to our "weaker brethren" and a stumbling block to those who turn to Christ (1 Corinthians 8:7-13), it could also lead to confusion among our children whom we seek to raise in the Christian faith. The Bible has clear records of the destruction of pagan altars upon our accepting Christ as Lord and Saviour (2 Chronicles 34:3b-7). Believers need not, however, be afraid of the presence of an altar in the home (should we not own the residence we are living in). We are victorious in Christ and the devil is a defeated foe.

Furthermore, the items on the altar are but dead pieces of wood or clay (Psalm 115:4-7). Christians should not be afraid of the possibility of being spiritually oppressed or possessed as a result of the mere presence of the altar. We are not to make offerings to the deceased or worship them, as God has commanded us to worship none but Him (Exodus 20:3-5).

An Alternative: A place in the home where our family photographs may be displayed, presents a good alternative. This allows for a break with Chinese religious practice, while preserving the memory of our dearly departed for our future generations and ourselves.

The Ancestral Tablet

Forty-nine days after a person dies, a rite is performed to invite one of the three souls that an individual is believed to possess, to inhabit the ancestral tablet. The presence of the tablet is thought to strengthen family solidarity, and bring blessing and protection to all in the family. It also serves as a reminder of the continued union between the living and the dead. The origin of the ancestral tablet is most commonly associated with *Mu Lian*, a mythological figure.

Mu Lian, it is told, was a very bad-tempered person who regularly beat up his mother over the slightest and smallest issues. While working in the fields one day, *Mu Lian* got tired and sat down for a break. As he rested under a tree, his eyes were drawn to a nest with a mother bird looking after its chicks. Led into a reflection of his life, *Mu Lian* began to realize how much he owed his mother and how much he had hurt her with his abuse. Just then, in the distance, he saw his mother coming with his afternoon meal. Sorry for the way he had treated his mother, *Mu Lian* began running towards her, intending to seek her forgiveness. When his mother saw him running towards her, however, she became afraid, thinking that he was coming to beat her up again, so she turned around and began running away from him. The more *Mu Lian* gave chase, the faster his mother ran, until she came to a large body of water and, in her desperation, jumped into it. *Mu Lian* jumped in after his mother to try to save her, but to no avail. All he could salvage was a piece of the wooden basket his mother had been carrying. This he took home, and upon it he carved the name of his mother in remembrance of her.

Biblical Approach: How are believers to view and treat the ancestral tablet? Is it simply an item for remembrance, or a place where part of the actual "essence" or soul of an ancestor resides, or something within which an evil spirit masquerading as our ancestor is present? As with the family altar mentioned earlier, we need have no fear of the ancestral altar. Apart from the fact that we have authority over the devil and his demonic minions (Luke 10:19) and victory in Christ (our names are written in heaven — Luke 10:20), the ancestral tablet is just a piece of carved wood (Psalm 115:4-7). The Bible also does not teach that an individual has three souls. Christians are not to make for themselves an ancestral tablet (Deuteronomy 27:15). Any such items in our possession should be removed (Acts 19:19), to avoid stumbling a fellow believer (1 Corinthians 8:9-13), and to please God (Deuteronomy 23:14). (For a fuller treatment of the issue, see Appendix E.)

An Alternative: A viable Christian alternative for the remembrance of our ancestor is the use of a photograph. This is a much better visual aid and has none of the religious connotations commonly attached to the ancestral tablet.

Offerings to the Dead

To some extent, this practice stems from the Buddhist concept of reincarnation and salvation through self-effort, which holds that the form of our rebirth is dependent upon the merit accumulated (in a previous life of which we have no memory). Merit may be transferred to aid our ancestors in their reincarnation to a higher form of life and entry into the Western Paradise, simply by making an offering in their name. Offerings are also made to gain favour with our ancestors, when the fulfilment of a need is sought, and to ensure a good and comfortable life for the deceased in the *Yin* World.

Biblical Approach: Upon a blending of the various religious concepts in practice, and the erosion over time of their original purpose and emphasis (something that happens to all traditions), the focus of Chinese ancestral worship as an act of filial piety gradually changed. In its place arose a fairly utilitarian practice that, while maintaining a semblance of filial piety, had the strong underlying notion of pleading with the ancestors for protection from the *kui* and for blessings.[19] Though this practice shows a belief in the afterlife, the concept of afterlife here is quite different from that taught by the Bible. Believers are not to get involved in this practice for a number of reasons. To begin with, the destiny of our ancestors is already sealed and offerings cannot buy them any merit. In addition, nothing may be expected from offerings to our ancestors, as it is God alone who blesses and provides for all our needs. Moreover, the connotation of worship attached to this practice is against the commands of God (Exodus 20:2-5).

Material Wealth

It is said that in the *Han* dynasty, money was buried with the dead. Later generations then developed the practice of giving departed spirits an offering of paper money ("hell bank notes"). This practice has been expanded in our modern age by, among other things, the offering of paper servants, cars, television sets, credit cards and DVD players. These offerings appear to go beyond the idea of transferring merit to the deceased. The perception here is that the nether world (the *Yin* World) functions along the same lines as our real world. Thus, among other things, money and luxuries are necessary to ensure the departed lives well and is not bullied in the nether world.[20]

Biblical Approach: A question raised by this practice is: Can spirits be bribed? If the *Yin* World is just like this world, where material possessions determine our state of "life", and where "money talks", then what is the point of life? Can money buy our salvation — both while we are alive and after we are dead? The Bible does not teach the need for these "amenities" in the afterlife, but it does teach that one should not cling to worldly treasures and material things (Matthew 19:16-21). Above all, it should be remembered that God provides for all our needs, and He cannot be bribed. Believers, therefore, need not, and should not, be involved in this practice.

Incense

The use of incense appears to have started from the later *Wei* dynasty (386-535 AD). Its introduction and use is generally derived from Buddhism,[21] and it is viewed as a Western import. In ancient days, others besides the Chinese also used incense in their worship. For example, in ancient Egypt, some engaged in a worship of trees, like the sandalwood tree, and as part of the worship, bark from this tree was burned. Much of the meaning behind the use of incense and joss sticks is lost to us. Most today take it simply as part of the practice associated with worship of the gods and veneration of our ancestors.

Biblical Approach: Ancient beliefs advocate that "the burning of incense was potent as an animating force, and especially as a giver of life to the dead, it came to be regarded as a divine substance in the sense that it had the power of resurrection."[22] Roman Catholics would not, generally, have a problem with believers holding joss sticks. Many Protestants would, however, say "no" to the holding of joss sticks and the offering of incense. This is because in the Bible, the offering of incense is always associated with prayer (Revelation 8:4), and prayer, like worship, is to be directed towards God alone. The Bible also records the destruction of pagan incense altars (2 Chronicles 34:3-7) as an act of separation from idolatry.

An Alternative: The practice of offering incense to our ancestors is to be avoided due to its connotation of worship (our worship is reserved for God alone). The lighting of a candle would serve as an adequate expression of remembrance (and only of remembrance) of our dearly departed.

Candles

Candles are commonly used in Chinese religious worship, probably as a result of the ancient practice of conducting the worship before dawn, when candles would be needed to illuminate the food that had been prepared as it lay exhibited at the east side of the worship hall.[23] Over the years, and probably out of expediency, many have taken the simple lighting and placing of two candles together, to signify the setting up of an altar.

Biblical Approach: There does not appear to be any religious significance to the use of candles in this manner by the Chinese. Candles lit in similar fashion have been used in the Church for centuries, probably for the same reason as the Chinese, and that is to provide lighting. Over time, the Church came to view the lighting of two candles as a reminder of Christ and the work He has done[24] (John 8:12; 2 Corinthians 4:4b). In the Roman Catholic church, candles are often lit in remembrance of the dead or to signify prayers being said for the dead.

An Alternative: There is no real religious significance to the use of candles. As candles appear in general use in most traditional religions (albeit with differing connotations), no restriction needs to be placed on Christians lighting a candle (in church or before a photograph of the deceased at home) in remembrance of the departed. With regard to whether or not the lighting of two candles constitutes the setting up of an altar, the question should be one of intent, and of the witness being presented. Within the church, the use of candles in worship has been given a Christian interpretation; it symbolizes the light of Christ that disperses darkness, the flames of Pentecost, the life of the assembled church, and the expectation of the eternal day.[25]

Food

In ancestral worship, food is often offered as a sign of the continued inter-dependence between the living and the dead. Over the centuries, many have also made these offerings in an attempt to "bribe" the spirits (our ancestors) so that they would bless us; the *kui* (hungry ghosts) so they would not harm us; and the ruling spirits of the *Yin* World so as to win merit for our ancestors. Most, however, do so simply in remembrance of the dead or in adherence to tradition.

Biblical Approach: The Bible does not teach a continued interdependence between the living and the dead. The stated reasons for the offering of food is contrary to our Christian belief, which advocates the sovereignty of a God who alone decides our fate and who is more than able to protect us from all evil, and provide for all our needs. As to the partaking of this food, Christians need to apply the principles laid out in 1 Corinthians 8 and 10. These two chapters do not speak of any danger or demonic efficacy in the offered food. Rather, they teach the need to separate oneself from any participation in pagan feasts and worship. (For a Biblical teaching on how believers are to treat food that has been offered to idols, see Appendix E.)

An Alternative: As a means of remembrance, the food best loved by the deceased may be prepared for the family on the anniversary of his passing. Stories concerning the departed may then be revived and imparted to the next generation as the significance of the food is explained. The food should not, however, be placed before any representation of the deceased, to avoid any allusion to worship.

CHAPTER 8

AN EVALUATION OF ANCESTRAL VENERATION

Ancestral Veneration Defined

In this section, a few terms used in reference to ancestral worship, as well as its basic tenet of filial piety, will be examined and discussed.

Veneration or Worship?

Are those who engage in ancestral worship involved in idolatry? Is this traditional Chinese practice purely an act of remembrance, or is it worship? The *New Expanded Webster's Dictionary* defines "veneration" as to revere (to regard with awe and respect) or to regard as sacred.[26] Note the thin line separating these two definitions and the ease with which one may move from one definition to the other. Those with an animistic perspective would have a hard time distinguishing between veneration as "awe and respect", and veneration as "to regard as sacred". For the Chinese, this is due to their animistic belief in spirits and a multiplicity of gods, to the point where no clear distinction may at times be made between *shen* (gods, immortals and ghosts), and *kui* (hungry ghosts and uncared for spirits or ancestors).

Biblical Approach: It is easier for Christians to make a distinction between the two definitions, as the Bible clearly states that we are to worship God alone, and none other (Exodus 20:1-6). Our ancestors may, therefore, be venerated only in the sense that they are remembered with respect (see Appendix C for a diagrammatic representation of the animistic and Christian scales of veneration). A major difficulty in the acceptance of the traditional Chinese practice of ancestral worship lies in that similar offerings are made, and prayers said, to gods and ghosts, deities and demons alike. The idea communicated is, therefore, one of worship, not respect and remembrance. With this in mind, let us realize that due to our human propensity to lean towards an animistic view of life, veneration of the deceased within the Christian context may easily develop into a viewing of the worthy as sacred.

Filial Piety

The practice of ancestral veneration spread rapidly as a result of the Confucian teaching on filial piety. Today, this theoretical basis has, in many practical ways, been superseded by Buddhist and Daoist beliefs in reincarnation and the *Dao* respectively (funeral rites and offerings for the gaining of merit, etc.). Filial piety is, nonetheless, still a major tenet of this practice. Confucius advocated that to establish the family, *li* (propriety — the observance of rites in the proper way and time) must be observed. This includes according propriety to our ancestors, who regulated the family life of their descendants. Having ordered the family, Confucius brought the wider society under the concept of filial piety by adjusting society to the role of the ancestral fathers, whose will take on the authority of a mandate from heaven. The five-fold social relationships advocated by Confucius are: ruler to minister; father to son; husband to wife; elder brother to younger brother; and friend to friend.

Biblical Approach: The basic thought, of honouring parents and ancestors, behind the concept of filial piety is quite acceptable to the Christian faith (Exodus 20:12). For example, it is important and good for Christians to learn to think in terms of the corporate body, and not only in terms of the individual. Not all expressions of the Confucian concept of filial piety, however, or the stated extent of the relationship between the living and the dead (for example, the continued inter-dependence between the two, and the offering of sacrifices as an integral part of filial piety) are acceptable. Christians should draw out what is good behind the concept of filial piety and apply it to their own relationships (for example, to honour and obey our parents, and to keep the memory of our dearly departed alive).

The Advocated Worldview[27]

The worldview advocated by ancestral veneration is that of a traditional animistic society, as opposed to that of a modern society. Of interest is how this practice has imbibed aspects of the latter worldview while maintaining a fair representation of the former in our rapidly modernizing world.

Distinctions between the Worldviews of Traditional and Modern Societies

First, traditional societies advocate a cyclical view of history (there is no sense of dating, and the world is looked upon as part of the cycle of nature). Modern societies, on the other hand, view history as moving in a certain progression (which results in a sense of purpose, direction and the passing of time). Second, traditional societies lack a personal consciousness (the ethic for living is set by societal values), whereas in a modern society, one is considered a moral, free individual capable of making one's own choices and decisions. Third, traditional societies view one's harmony with nature as the highest achievement. Modern societies, though, consider the realization of one's personhood to be the highest achievement. Fourth, traditional societies advocate a dualism between God and creation, with God being a supernatural being distinct from nature. Modern societies, however, generally view God to be a part of the "total reality" (the very essence of reality within creation).

Like traditional societies, the Chinese society tends to focus on its own people and land. The emphasis of its social structure, however, on harmony and each knowing his place in society has allowed for the growth of a complex and extensive society. As the Chinese society absorbed new ideas into its existing worldview, it progressed from a traditional society to a rich and complex civilization.

Biblical Approach: The practice of ancestral veneration propagates a traditional worldview, some aspects of which are acceptable to the Christian faith, while others are not. The traditional view of history as meaningless and fatalistic is contrary to Christian beliefs. The modern view of the progression of history is more in line with our belief that God has created us with a purpose, and is continuing His work in the world today to achieve this purpose. While it is good that societal values play a role in our lives (giving one a sense of corporate responsibility), a total lack of personal consciousness is bad (no sense of guilt develops when there is no sense of personal responsibility). The concepts of highest achievement advocated by both worldviews have some validity as they teach ideas advocated by the Bible. The traditional view creates a respect for and the sense of a need to preserve nature (Christian stewardship of the earth — Genesis 1:26-30), while the modern worldview gives one a sense of personal identity (the creation of men and women in the image of God — Genesis 1:26a).

The dualistic view advocated by traditional societies implies the possibility of breaking away from God. Thus arises the concept of the *Yin* World. The monistic notion (that there is no distinction between God and creation) advocated by modern societies makes no distinction between the Christian goal and the goal of non-believers. There is, therefore, no concept of the *Yin* World, as there can be no separation from God (a universalist viewpoint).

An Alternative: A Christian worldview must be developed — one that draws from the best that is biblical in the worldviews of both the traditional and modern societies.

Eternal Life

Eternal life has been given to all believers, past and present, by God, simply through the acceptance of Jesus Christ as their personal Lord and Saviour (John 3:16; 1 John 5:11). As eternal life basically means "the life of the age to come", it implies "not only ever-lastingness, but a quality of life derived from relationship with Christ (John 17:3; Romans 6:23)."[28] Experienced in part in this present age, this life will find full expression only at the consummation of the age. Though death marks a discontinuity between this life and the next, the eternal life we have in Christ "guarantees a continuity of relationship to Christ even through death". Before the return of Christ, we are at death, taken up to the bosom of Abraham (Luke 16:22) or Paradise (Luke 23:43). Nothing, however, is mentioned in the Bible as to what this place is physically like, or where it might be. The fact that believers who have passed away are currently residing in the bosom of Abraham implies the possibility of our continued relationship with them. This is due to the fact that, though dead, they have not been totally annihilated, but are simply awaiting the return of Christ in a certain place prepared for them by the Lord.

Communion of Saints

In Christianity, we have a Doctrine of the Communion of Saints, a theological concept that refers to the fellowship of "believers": earthbound believers with each other, earthbound believers with the saints in heaven, and the saints in heaven with each other. It is easy for us to understand the fellowship between earthbound believers and that between the saints in heaven, but what of the idea that earthbound believers may be or are in fellowship with the saints in heaven? Technically, it means that the saints in heaven and we who are alive, being equally part of the body of Christ, are in fellowship with one another. Does this mean, then, that we can communicate with the dead, or that the dead can communicate with us? Is this what this doctrine advocates? No, it is not.

The Doctrine of the Communion of Saints does not advocate that people should pray to the saints, though it has been interpreted as such in some Anglo-Catholic and Roman Catholic circles.[29] This doctrine, generally interpreted according to the dimensions of both time and space, simply reminds us that all believers past, present and future, are equally a part of the body of Christ.[30] Its worth lies primarily in its expression of the unity of all believers (past and present), the willing employment of the gifts of God for the salvation and need of other saints, and the common salvation history current saints share with those of the past. Ours (saints past, present and future) is a bond of fellowship arising from a shared heritage of redemption.[31]

Communication with the Dead

Those who believe and engage in ancestral worship hold that we may communicate with the dead, either directly as prayers are offered before the ancestral tablet or indirectly through a medium. Luke 16:19-31 tells the parable[32] of a poor man named Lazarus and a rich man who, upon their death, went to the bosom of Abraham and *Hades* respectively. From *Hades*, the rich man pleaded with Abraham to have Lazarus visit his relatives and warn them of the consequences. This parable points to a gulf between the bosom of Abraham and *Hades* (Luke 16:26). We get the impression that those locked up in *Hades* are unable to leave or communicate with those in the realm of the living, whereas those in the bosom of Abraham are potentially able to do so (Luke 16:27-31). We must, however, be careful not to read too much into Luke 16:19-31 because as a parable, it is not primarily meant to reveal to us how the spirit world functions.

What about the passage of the Bible that speaks of Saul visiting the witch of *Endor* to have her call up Samuel from the dead (1 Samuel 28)? Did Samuel really rise from the dead? Does this event give us licence to visit witches and mediums to call up our dearly departed? To answer these questions, we must have a right understanding of this passage. To begin, let us delve into the question of whether or not Samuel literally and physically rose from the dead. Many, not wanting to give credit to the witch, have dogmatically argued that this "apparition" was not Samuel, but a demonic imitation. If we read this story carefully, we would have to say that it was Samuel himself who appeared before Saul and not some demonic imitation (1 Samuel 28:12-19). Before we develop this point further, consider the reaction of the witch at the appearance of Samuel (1 Samuel 28:12).

The witch was surprised and shocked. If she really had the power and authority to call up the dead, why was she so frightened? She should have been quite used to such an occurrence. There was shock and fear because she had not expected Samuel to actually appear, being more accustomed to vague demonic impressions. So, to the question of whether or not witches and mediums have the power to call up or communicate with the dead, the answer is "no". The Bible is clear in stating that these people have no such ability, but have, in fact, been deceived by the devil, and are communicating only with demonic impersonations. I believe that Samuel (not some demonic impersonation) actually appeared before Saul; remember nothing is impossible with God. If our Lord desires and wills it, the dead may appear before us, as Samuel appeared to Saul, and Moses and Elijah to Christ (Matthew 17:1-3).

The issue for us, however, is not the appearance of the dead to the living. Rather, it is whether or not God allows such a thing to happen. Leviticus 19:31 and Deuteronomy 18:9-13 make it clear that we are not to attempt to call up or communicate with the dead. Those who do so defile themselves and are "detestable to the Lord". They are actually engaged in the occult and as such, place themselves under bondage to the devil. 1 Samuel 28:8-19 is an exception rather than a rule, for the incident took place within a special context for the fulfilment of the divine purpose of God. The ban on engaging in witchcraft to communicate with the dead stands, and 1 Samuel 28 cannot be taken as a proof text for consulting mediums. Christians must disengage themselves from all practices of divination and witchcraft (Deuteronomy 18:10-13).

E. John Hamlin, in his commentary on Isaiah, notes that there are three main reasons for the prohibition against any attempt to communicate with the dead.[33] First, people are mistaken in believing that the dead have powers, because they do not (Genesis 3:19; Isaiah 14:10). Second, communicating with the dead leads to great distress, because the motive of those seeking to do so often stems from a selfish desire for supernatural blessings and aid (Isaiah 8:21,22). Third, necromancy (consulting with the dead) is forbidden because it turns people away from God and towards themselves (Deuteronomy 18:11,12; Isaiah 8:19,20).

General Evaluation

The traditional Chinese practice of ancestral veneration is syncretistic, with no clear line drawn between acts of reverence and respect, and acts of worship. Much of that which constitutes the practice of ancestral worship is steeped in religious and superstitious beliefs and practices. Sound biblical discernment, therefore, must be exercised with regard to this practice to determine that which is acceptable to our Christian faith. Rightly advocated and encouraged are the concepts of filial piety and social responsibility of mankind. The family unit is truly something Christians must diligently work to maintain, uphold and build. The individualistic attitude so common in our world today must be tempered with a sense of our corporate relationship with and responsibility towards others.

Though ancestral worship is not to be practised by believers, we should, nonetheless, learn the need to remember our dearly departed with thanksgiving. It is good for Christians to raise their children to remember their ancestors, as this would aid not only in the development of solidarity within the family, but also in the passing on (to the next generation) of the Christian faith. An education in the faith within the context of the home is one means of propagating the faith that is greatly lacking in the Christian community today.

Traditional Chinese Medicine

Chapter 9
Traditional Chinese Cures

General Observations

Alternative medicine is all the rage these days, as people find no relief in Western medical care for traditional ailments like cancer and a growing number of new diseases like Aids. There is also a turning back to traditional remedies, due to "a strong back-to-nature movement and rising demand for natural, herbal-based medicine and health products as an alternative to chemical-based medicine and adverse side effects."[1] In search of health and healing, more and more are turning to traditional remedies like herbal medicine and acupuncture, in the hope of finding a cure for their ailments. For these reasons, major pharmaceutical companies (like Merck, and Johnson & Johnson) are engaged in research into the traditional treatments of Latin America and Asia, in the hope that some cure may be discovered for the many ailments that afflict people today. Governments are also sitting up and taking note, with some, like Malaysia, even declaring traditional folk medicine to be part of the health care system of the nation.[2] Many hospitals, too, have departments and research centres experimenting at integrating traditional remedies with Western medical practice.

In actual fact, many traditional remedies have been around for decades, and in the Chinese context, even centuries. The situation simply is that these remedies have, in the last century, been pushed aside in the light of the overwhelming advance of Western medical science. Culturally, however, many non-Westerners have continued to rely on their respective traditional cures. For one thing, traditional remedy has been handed down from generation to generation. When our parents fell sick, they were fed with and "cured" by these remedies; what was good for them must be good for us. For another, Western medical science may not be readily accessible to these people, and even if it is, the cost may be beyond affordable means. In general, it is to be acknowledged that traditional Chinese medical care has been the mainstay and only form of healthcare in China for centuries, and its practice has helped many over the years.

Traditional Chinese cures are generally non-intrusive in that they do not, unlike Western medical science, incorporate surgery (to remove the appendix or transplant an organ, etc). This is not to say that traditional Chinese cures are better or worse than Western medical science. No judgement is being made here, except to note that each has its merits. Chinese medical care is also deemed non-intrusive in the sense that all cures prescribed are derived from "natural" elements, that is to say, herbs and *Da Qi*, etc, which rests in sharp contrast to "more intrusive" Western treatments, like chemotherapy, for example. This is another selling point of traditional Chinese cures. With a resurgence of interest in traditional cures and remedies, Christians need to ask and consider what our response should be? What is acceptable and what is unacceptable? In the pages to follow, I will endeavour to provide some answers.

The Influence of Daoism

Daoism is a major influence in Chinese medical science because of its fundamental belief in and recognition of the use of alchemy, rites and charms as a means of ensuring the right and good flow of *qi* in our lives for good health and the attainment of immortality. Ask most Chinese about the use of rites and charms for health, and you will probably hear a story of how a sick person is brought before a Daoist priest. The priest would then perform a rite, burn and dissolve a charm in some water, and give this concoction to the person to drink. Chinese medical science believes, as the Daoists do, that the right and unrestricted flow of *qi* through our bodies is essential for good health. It is generally believed that we may absorb *qi* from the food we eat, and from *qigong* exercises, which also help to maintain a proper circulation of *qi* in our bodies.

The belief is also held that certain elements of the earth have a greater ability to absorb and conduct *qi*, for example, jade and gold. Notice that many Chinese like to wear jade. This trend was established because of the belief that jade, as one of the best conductors of *qi*, will help those wearing it to absorb *qi* into the body, thus strengthening the physical constitution. It is thought that the jade will grow greener the longer one wears it, and this is a sign of it absorbing and accumulating *qi*. As the Chinese believe that one of the three souls of the departed resides in the corpse, the dead may still benefit from the wearing of jade. For some past emperors of China, this belief led to the creation of a burial suit made from head to toe of jade.

Biblical Approach: Christians hold no belief in *qi*, or the ability of jade and gold to conduct and channel *qi*. Sickness befalls us because we live in a sinful world full of diseases, some of which are caused by man (arising from our pollution of the environment, for example). Health and strength belong to us as we exercise and learn to eat healthily. Most, if not all, physicians will tell us that while they can help treat an ailment, they cannot heal a person. God, our Creator, is the only one who can heal, so Christians are to call upon Him whenever they fall sick. The Bible teaches us to call upon the elders of the church to pray for us whenever we fall sick (James 5:14,15). This is not to say that we should not, therefore, approach doctors for treatment, but that we are simply to pray in faith. There are some Christians who choose to forgo medical care, and a friend of mine almost died as a result of this fallacious teaching. Suffering from epilepsy, he was told to stop all medication and believe in God for healing. Desiring to be a man of faith, he did as encouraged and almost died from it as he subsequently suffered two epileptic seizures.

Christians, be wise. Know that our Lord God has given medical science to humanity, and to seek treatment from a doctor is not a sign of a lack of faith. What is important is that we learn not to look to doctors for healing, but to God. In addition, we must also persevere in prayer for healing, but leave the decision as to whether or not we will be healed in the hands of God, trusting that He knows what is best for us (2 Samuel 12; Acts 12). When we fall sick, treatment should be sought from doctors for physiological or biological problems and their causes, and prayers made to seek a healing touch from God.

The *Yin-Yang* Diagnostic Principle

There is a fundamental difference in how Western-trained doctors and Chinese *sinsehs* (doctors) diagnose their patients. For example, when we visit a doctor, he would check our blood pressure, listen to our heartbeat and breathing, and examine any physical symptoms of illness. A Chinese *sinseh* would also examine the physical symptoms, but he would draw much information for a diagnosis by simply feeling our pulse. By taking the pulse at different points (see Figure 7: The 12 Pulses of Ancient Chinese Medicine), he is deemed to be able to diagnose exactly which organ in our body is infected with disease and in need of treatment. Note that 10 of the 12 pulse points refer to actual organs within our bodies, that is, the small intestine, heart, gall bladder, bladder, kidney, liver, lung, spleen, stomach and large intestine. The other two pulse points refer not to physical organs within our bodies, but to two "spiritual organs", the pericardium and the triple warmer.

Figure 7: The 12 Pulses of Ancient Chinese Medicine[3]

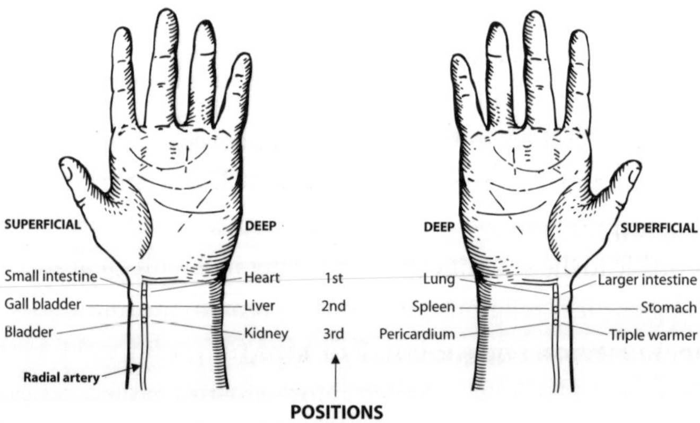

A Western-trained doctor, having been taught the biological and physiological make-up of human beings, will make a diagnosis based on this understanding. A Chinese *sinseh* is taught differently, and would as such, diagnose a patient on the basis of the *yin-yang* philosophy, on which much of Chinese medical science rests. *Yin* and *yang* are viewed as the two fundamental forces of the cosmos that generate all transformation in the universe.[4] A Chinese *sinseh* is taught that there are 12 meridians or *jing luo* in our human body along which *qi* flows (see Appendix G). These meridians do not conform to human physiology, but are unseen supernatural conduits of *qi*. The belief is that when we breathe, we do not just breathe in air, but we also breathe in *qi*. The *qi* is then disseminated throughout the body via the *jing luo*. Sickness occurs when the smooth and free flow of *qi* along the *jing luo* is disrupted, or when there is insufficient *qi* in the body.

Biblical Approach: There is no physiological or biological basis for the Chinese medical belief in the *jing luo* and the *yin-yang* diagnostic principle, as well as in the practice of feeling for the 12 pulses. There is even less basis for any belief in the ability to *dian xue*, which is the skill to stop the flow of *qi* along certain points of the 12 meridians in the body. Attempts today to divorce the diagnostic and treatment process from the Daoist principles and the concept of *yin* and *yang* that undergird it, to make it more acceptable to the scientific mind, have not met with great success. So long as these religious philosophies remain the foundation of Chinese medical science, it will be hard for traditional Chinese treatments to be fully accepted into mainstream medical practice, and in the same vein be acceptable to Christians. I would not encourage believers to become *sinsehs*, because those who choose to do so would in all probability have to first buy into the religious philosophies behind traditional Chinese medical practices. This said, are believers allowed to visit *sinsehs* for treatment? My personal advice is for us to avoid these visits as they communicate our belief in the religious philosophies behind the diagnosis. In addition, the treatments prescribed may well be linked to religious philosophies, and are of themselves, of uncertain efficacy.

Traditional Medical Treatments

Having diagnosed the problem, there are five basic approaches to therapy open to the *sinseh*. In most cases, the treatment would encompass a combination of two or more of these five standard therapies, which are the treatment of the spirit, dietary therapy, medicinal therapy, massage and acupuncture.

The treatment of the spirit stems from the belief that ill health results when we fall out of harmony with the *Da Qi* of the universe. When so diagnosed, the treatment recommended is for the patient to engage in meditation, where the sick is guided towards the *Dao* in the practice of a modest and tranquil way of life. The meditation is drawn from Daoist and Buddhist practice and philosophy, and is said to help a patient lower his heart and breathing rate, as well as blood pressure. In dietary therapy, a patient is directed towards eating or abstaining from certain foods. It is a belief that some foods contain more *yin qi* and others more *yang qi*, the imbalance of which causes ill health. The *sinseh* will, therefore, prescribe the right food to eat, depending on whether the patient lacks *yin qi* or *yang qi*. In general, ladies are deemed to comprise more of *yin qi* and men, *yang qi*.

Medicinal therapy refers to the prescribing of herbal remedies to clear blockages and allow a better flow of *qi* along the *jing luo* within us. More will be said of herbal remedies in the next section. Massages are another form of treatment prescribed. These massages, though, are unlike those of the West in that they are not meant solely to relieve sore and tense muscles. Massages in Chinese medical treatment, while they do serve such a purpose, are primarily meant to clear blockages in the *jing luo,* and help circulate and re-establish the right and smooth flow of *qi* within us. Should it be diagnosed that these massages may not clear the blockages encountered, the *sinseh* would then prescribe the last and most intrusive of treatments available to Chinese medical science, and that is acupuncture. In the pages to follow, we will delve further into the practice of acupuncture.

Biblical Approach: In general, it may be said that Western medical science is part medicinal (the taking of medicine and pills) and part surgical. Chinese medical science is generally part medicinal (the taking of herbal remedies) and part religious (compare its diagnostic practice). You will note that the five basic treatments available to the *sinseh* all have to do with the restoration of a right balance and flow of *qi* within us. This is something the Bible does not teach, and we, as believers, are not to subscribe to it. The use of Daoist and Buddhist meditative techniques in the treatment of the spirit, in particular, is something believers should have nothing to do with. Some might, however, want to argue the point that we may apply some of the treatments — for example, herbal therapies and massages — without reference to the religious philosophies behind them. In response, let us note the warning of Dr *Zhang Xiaorui* of the traditional medicine programme of the World Health Organization, that Westerners might not make the best use of the traditional treatments. She states, "One problem is that they ignore the philosophy that accompanies it in China."[5] To divorce the philosophies behind the treatments from the actual treatments themselves renders them ineffective. Not doing so causes us to compromise our faith. As Christians, the choice is clear.

Herbal Remedies

Herbal remedies are part of most, if not all, tribal societies worldwide, from the Americas to Europe to Africa and Asia, and the practice of Chinese herbal medicine is over 4,000 years old. Deriving medicine from herbs and plants is an age-old practice that we should not look down upon. The common everyday aspirin, for example, is derived from the willow tree, and the two cancer drugs, taxanes and camptothecines, from the yew and *kiju* trees respectively.[6] An anti-malaria drug called artemisinin, has also been derived from the traditional herb used by the Chinese to combat malaria, that is, the *qing hau su*.[7] Today, major pharmaceutical companies pump huge amounts of money and resources into exploring traditional herbal remedies, in the hope of discovering new treatments and cures for both traditional and the growing number of new diseases inflicting humanity.

State of Current Research

Those engaged in researching traditional herbal remedies for a cure are faced with a number of issues that make their task doubly difficult. To begin with, most herbal remedies do not focus on the consumption of any single herb, but are usually a combination of three or more varieties of herbs. Moreover, these herbal concoctions, even for the same ailment, may vary from individual to individual, depending on the diagnosis of the differing cause in each individual. In relation to this, a different combination of herbs would also be prescribed for males and females suffering from the same ailment, because of the view that males have more *yang qi*, and females, *yin qi*. The herbs prescribed must, therefore, be different, so a female suffering from a lack of *yin qi* and an abundance of *yang qi*, for example, might not be prescribed herbs to boost the presence of *yang qi* in her. Doing so would not heal, but only serve to aggravate her illness. Furthermore, another hindrance to finding a cure in traditional Chinese herbal medicine is the fact that it is often combined with other treatments, like acupuncture. These difficulties make it hard for researchers to isolate the one true cure for the ailment being treated.

Biblical Approach: Herbs are real physical elements and do, as such, have redemptive properties within them, as have been stated above with regard to certain Western medicine that has been derived from herbs and plants. In general, Christians need have no objections to partaking of herbal remedies. Our objection, in any case, is not to the herbal remedies, but the diagnostic process (see discussion above) by which the combination of herbs is prescribed (for example, the *yin* and *yang* make-up of females and males), and the religious philosophical rationale given for their efficacy. In any event, it is not possible for us to place total trust in herbal remedies, as what works for one person may not work as well, if at all, for another, because of the difficulty involved in isolating a specific chemical cure from traditional Chinese herbal remedy. In addition, even if we are able to isolate the herb, unless the chemical within it that provides the cure is properly distilled and made into a pill or solution, we might not yet take a sufficient amount of the drug to effect healing. For example, there needs to be an exact measurement of the chemical required and a difference in dosages for adults and infants.

Acupuncture

The word "acupuncture" is derived from the Latin *acu* (with a needle) or *acus* (needle), and *pungere* (to sting). First introduced in Europe in the seventeenth century, it has been practised in one form or another for over 5,000 years. Its actual origin, however, is lost in history. The goal of classical acupuncture therapy is to correct the imbalance of *yin* and *yang* by stimulating specific points along the *jing luo*, thereby draining excess *qi*, or restoring any deficiency of *qi*. On occasion, burning *moxa*, a concoction made from the mugwort herb, is wrapped around the acupuncture needle inserted into the body. This herb is believed to have medicinal value, while the heat that emanates from burning it on the needle is said to help relieve pain.

The Claims of Practitioners

Many medical benefits have been attributed to the practice of acupuncture, one of which is that it is an alternative to the normal chemical anaesthesia employed by Western medical science. Practitioners claim that acupuncture may be used effectively as an anaesthetic for major surgery. Professor *Cao Xiaoding*, director of the Institute of Acupuncture Research and Centre of Clinical Pain Research of the *Shanghai* Medical University, recalls having observed in 1964 "an unusual chest surgery in *Shanghai*, which used acupuncture in place of an anaesthetic." In her words, "It was a stunning feat involving a team of three acupuncturists, who worked on 20 pairs of acupressure points."[8] Research conducted by Professor *Cao* and her team of researchers, however, has shown that different people react differently to acupuncture. While it relaxes and raises the skin temperature in some, it causes the opposite effect in others.

Another claim concerns the ability of practitioners to *dian xue*. From time to time in the *wuxia pian* (Chinese sword-fighting movies) we watch, there would be scenes where *kung fu* exponents are shown to perform the *dian xue* skill. This is the skill of stopping the flow of *qi* along certain points of the different *jing luo* so as to achieve various effects. Press one point along a *jing luo*, and a person would be stopped from moving. Press another along the same *jing luo* and a person might be killed. Press a point along another *jing luo* and a person could be made mute, or caused to laugh or cry for as long as that point is sealed or blocked. Though we find this happening only in movies, there is a belief that it can actually be done. It is not practised today simply because the skill has been lost and no one knows how to go about exercising it.

Scientific Acknowledgement

In 1979, the World Health Organization held an inter-regional seminar on acupuncture in *Beijing*, in the course of which a provisional list of diseases that could be treated by acupuncture was drawn up (see Figure 8: Provisional List of Treatable Diseases). The World Health Organization, however, also noted this list to be based on clinical experience (day-to-day observations of the effects of acupuncture), and not necessarily research (systematic and carefully controlled experimentation of test subjects).[9] At the time, the World Health Organization also "warned that acupuncture should not be used during pregnancy, in tumours, in skin infections and when the patient has a cardiac pacemaker". In addition to this provisional endorsement by the World Health Organization, the Food and Drug Administration of the United States of America in March

Figure 8: Provisional List of Treatable Diseases[10]

Diseases of the upper respiratory tract	Acute sinusitis, acute rhinitis, common cold, acute tonsillitis
Diseases of the respiratory system	Acute bronchitis, bronchial asthma (in children)
Disorders of the eye	Acute conjunctivitis, central retinitis, myopia (in children), cataract (without complications)
Disorders of the mouth	Toothache, gingivitis, acute and chronic pharyngitis
Gastro-intestinal disorders	Chronic duodenal ulcer (pain relief), acute duodenal ulcer (without complications), hiccough, acute and chronic gastritis, acute bacillary dysentery, constipation, diarrhoea
Neurological and muscular-skeletal disorders	Headache, migraine, facial palsy, neurogenic bladder dysfunction, nocturnal enuresis, tennis elbow, sciatica, lower back pain, osteoarthritis

1996 recognized and classified acupuncture needles as medical devices (similar to a syringe and a scalpel) for "general use" by trained personnel.

Explanations for the Efficacy of Acupuncture

For practitioners of acupuncture, its efficacy rests in the restoration of the smooth flow of *qi* in our *jing luo*. What is the opinion of medical doctors and scientists? Do we know the real medical, physiological or biological cause of the efficacy of acupuncture? Trained medical personnel suggest that a stimulation of the nerves by acupuncture needles results in the release of chemical and natural painkillers within our bodies called endorphins. Professor *Cao* believes that "the sensation of the needle — a sore, swelling and numbing sensation — acts on the pain-modulating system in the brain, which releases an opiate peptide" that suppresses pain.[11] Another theory suggests that the stimulation of nerves by acupuncture needles results in the transmission of electrical impulses to the spinal cord and lower centres of the brain, and thence to the diseased area. The former is the more widely accepted and promoted theory. The latter is not so widely held because the points at which acupuncture needles are inserted do not always conform anatomically to any major nerves of our nervous system. On the whole, the situation is that no one really knows the true cause of the efficacy of acupuncture.

Biblical Approach: Addressing the practice of acupuncture based purely on the religious philosophy behind it, believers must conclude that its efficacy has a demonic root. The rationale behind such an answer rests in the fact that the philosophy behind the practice of acupuncture is contrary to the teaching of the Bible.

This being the case, the logic follows that any supernatural force called upon or harnessed by the practice of acupuncture cannot be from God. What then are we saying? That the whole practice of acupuncture is demonic? Is there no redemptive aspect to acupuncture at all? The philosophy that undergirds the practice of acupuncture is religious in nature (drawn largely from Daoism). To have nothing to do with this philosophy means first that we should not study to be an acupuncturist. In any case, a believer would find it hard to engage in the practice of acupuncture. For example, I know an acupuncturist, now a Christian, who struggles with the continued practice of acupuncture, for the simple reason that all he has been taught, about how a diagnosis is to be carried out and treatments prescribed, runs contrary to the teachings of the Christian faith.

Medically speaking, it has been acknowledged that there are medical benefits to acupuncture (see above), but research is still being conducted into the exact extent and nature of these benefits. The problem simply is that we cannot fully explain why certain things happen when an acupuncture needle is inserted into us, though it is quite commonly accepted that something does happen. As research is still ongoing, it is too early for us to say for certain whether or not acupuncture has any true benefits and properties that may be redeemed for medical science. For believers, it is clear enough that the philosophy that undergirds the practice of acupuncture (the flow of *qi* along the *jing luo*, for example) is to be unquestionably and totally rejected, and regarded as unredeemable. While we might reserve judgement on the possible medical benefit/s that might arise from its practice, we should recognize that the only real benefit it may afford us is that of it being another and a non-chemical form of anaesthesia.

The question most people would then ask is this: Though I cannot be an acupuncturist, considering the possibility of redemptive medical benefits of acupuncture, can I simply visit an acupuncturist for treatment? This is a tricky question! Believers, who hold strongly to the idea that acupuncture has dubious underpinnings due to the emphasis on the supernatural channelling of *qi*, are clear that they should avoid seeking treatment from an acupuncturist. The concern is that we might, in the process, become spiritually oppressed. Though I myself have no plans or desire to visit an acupuncturist for treatment, I am keeping an open mind as I await the results of medical research into acupuncture. I do not believe in the religious philosophy that undergirds its practice, or in all its claims of efficacy, but I do believe that it may have some medical benefit. In addition, I do not subscribe to the idea that believers may be spiritually oppressed simply because they visit or receive treatment from an acupuncturist.

Our Lord God is greater and more than able to protect us from demonic influences. The issue, I believe, lies not in our visiting or receiving treatment from an acupuncturist, but in our weakness of faith that sees us buying into and believing the religious and supernatural philosophy behind the practice. Furthermore, there is the greater danger that in our search for healing and health, we may lose sight of God and forsake our trust and belief in Him. As we look around for alternative cures, let us ask ourselves these questions: To what extent are we prepared to go to gain healing and health for ourselves, and our loved one/s? Where do we draw the line in our search for a cure? What if it is the will of God that we live with the ailment we now face? Remember how the apostle Paul prayed three times to be delivered from an affliction, yet it remained. In the process, Paul was taught humility and witnessed the strength of God made manifest and perfect in his life (2 Corinthians 12:7ff).

The story goes of a man who was greatly handicapped and suffered constant pain, for which there was no relief. A few days before he passed away a pastor visited him in the hospital and stated the obvious, that the man must be suffering terribly. The man replied that he was, and also that he did not blame God for his suffering. Rather, he shared that he looked upon the suffering as an opportunity to come before God, to sit at His feet to learn and grow in the spiritual disciplines. God is more than able to meet our desire for healing and health. What He desires, however, is not that we receive a quick fix to all our problems, but that we develop an attitude of thanksgiving and trust in God regardless of what we may face. All said and done, I would not personally direct people to an acupuncturist, simply because the efficacy of the treatment received is dubious. Do your best in the search for healing and health, but always remember to put your trust solely in God and your life in His hands.

Chapter 10

The Mystical Practice of *Qigong*

Claims of Efficacy

Watch *wuxia pian* (Chinese sword-fighting movies) and you would undoubtedly encounter at some point or other in the movie, someone trying to heal the internal injuries of another person by seeking to transfer his *qi* into the poisoned or injured party. You would probably also find in these movies one or two elderly individuals who either look very much younger than they actually are (a 100-year-old looking half his age), or are in better health than they should be for their age (a centenarian with great strength and vitality).

While most may consider this merely storytelling, practitioners of *qigong* claim that mental and physical healing may be achieved through breathing exercises, meditation (to reach a quiescent state) and physical exercises of *qigong*. *Qigong* is said to play an active role in preventing and treating diseases, protecting and strengthening our constitution, resisting premature aging and senility, and prolonging life.[12] *Qigong* has been practised in China for centuries and remains widely practised today. Nonetheless, concerns have been expressed by the secular press with regard to the efficacy of the practice of *qigong*. Part of one such report taken from the *China Daily* (6 June 1990) reads:

> "Some self-proclaimed *qigong* masters are quacks, and many *qigong* devotees have practised *qigong* to excess, sometimes with alarming results. Over the past two years, the mental hospitals of China have reportedly admitted thousands of people suffering from hallucinations and other mental problems that have arisen in the course of practicing *qigong*...One report told of a woman with a seemingly pathological commitment to *qigong*, who grew increasingly distraught, and began hearing an imaginary voice telling her to 'kill everybody in the world'. She attacked her 70-year-old mother and neighbours had to intervene...Some of these 'masters' tell their students they should strive to hear inaudible sounds and communicate with invisible spirits. *Qigong* followers with a strong desire for success may overdo it and 'approach insanity', a psychiatrist from *Anding* Hospital in *Beijing* was quoted as saying."

Biblical Approach: The Bible does not teach that we may attain health and the prolongation of life through any human means. God is the only one able to empower, heal and give life. We do note, however, that the Bible does have records of those with superhuman strength to break chains, etc, but it is taught that these physical abilities are the result of demon possession and not some form of martial art (Matthew 8:28; Mark 5:1ff). The Bible teaches that when a person manifests some supernatural power or ability, the source of it is either God or the devil. In reflecting on the claims of the practitioners of *qigong*, we must ask ourselves from where do the supernatural ability and power come. As the Bible does not teach that there is *Da Qi* (vital breath) in the universe, and as God the Holy Spirit is not said to empower humans in the manner claimed by the practitioners of *qigong*, there can be only one other source.

Background to *Qigong* and *Qi*

The practice of *qigong* has a history in China of over 2,000 years and may be viewed as a Chinese form of yoga. *Qigong* is based on the ancient Chinese view of man and the universe as part of the *Dao*. To understand *qigong* and its practice, therefore, we must first understand the underlying concept of *qi*. This is important because the main characteristics of *qigong* include the training of essential *qi* in the human body, which integrates mental activity with body postures and respiration.[13]

Definition of *Qi*

Qi is *Dao* in action and *Da Qi* is the vital breath or great vitality (energy) that animates the cosmos — a universal, invisible energy or life force that flows through all living organisms. It is held that all creation exists in *qi*, and *qi* is within all creation. It is believed that the entire universe — and the human body (viewed as a microcosm of the universe) — is formed of the *Yin-Yang* forces and the Five Elements of Fire, Metal, Wood, Earth and Water (see Appendix F). A harmonious balance of these forces and elements must be maintained for the well-being of mankind and the universe. All creation requires the presence of *qi* within it in order to survive. In Chinese belief, food is one means by which *qi* may be absorbed, as what we eat is part of creation, and equally linked with and full of *qi*.

The Practice of *Qigong*

Practitioners of *qigong* believe that it is not enough for *qi* to be present in our lives. It must also flow freely and without interruption in the proper *jing luo* in our bodies, and the *qi* within us must be in harmony with the universe. If this is achieved, a person would remain healthy, but should something block the free flow of *qi*, then a person would fall sick. It is held that the person who knows how to circulate his *qi* maintains his own person and banishes all evil that might serve to harm him.[14] In *qigong*, what a practitioner tries to do is not just order and maintain the free and right flow of *qi* within the body, but also attempt to absorb more of the *Da Qi*. This is the two-fold purpose of the physical exercises — for example, the rubbing of our navel (a point through which *qi* may be absorbed into our bodies) — associated with *qigong*. The central place and importance of breath control and breathing exercises in the practice of *qigong* is due to the belief that one may inhale *qi* with air. It is believed that the "coarse" *qi* inhaled may be transformed by the adept into the "subtle" *qi* of heaven, and channelled to various parts of the body to promote health. In addition, this "subtle" *qi* may even be channelled to other people to help effect healing and health in them.

Biblical Approach: The Bible does not teach that there is *qi* in the universe. Neither does it teach that a human being is made of *qi*, and may absorb and transform the "coarse" *qi* inhaled into "subtle" *qi* that may be used for the betterment of life. The Bible does not teach that we are to seek to be filled with *qi*, but with the Holy Spirit (Ephesians 5:18ff). Believers are not to hold any belief in the concept of *qi* and, by extension, are not to engage in *qigong*, as any who engage in *qigong* must naturally buy into its underlying philosophy. A person may argue that there is no harm in engaging in the purely physical breathing and meditative exercises, for even psychologists encourage simple breathing exercises to help people relieve stress. In response, why not simply learn the non-religious breathing exercises to relieve stress? Why must we insist on practising the breathing exercises taught under *qigong*? In addition, we must question the meditative exercises taught, as they are drawn largely from Daoist and Buddhist religious traditions. The Bible encourages us to draw aside and spend time with God in quiet contemplation, but the call is for us to meditate on the teachings of God (Joshua 1:8), and none other.

An Alternative: *Qigong* is not the only means of ensuring that we maintain good health and a good sense of balance as we age. In any event, I do believe that the effectiveness of *qigong* rests primarily in the fact that it causes people to exercise their bodies and minds daily, two very important requirements for maintaining health as we age, and even while young. Alternatively, it has been a dream of mine that one day, a Christian would step up and develop an exercise regimen clearly divorced from any idolatrous philosophy of life. I believe such a regimen would need to have some of the following characteristics: To begin with, the movements must be slow (so the elderly can participate), and emphasize low impact (so stiff and aging joints are not damaged) and balance (an important requirement for the aging). Next, the exercises must be done standing up and be suitable for use by both an individual and a group. Moreover, the exercises must impact our cardio-vascular system, with the whole regimen flowing seamlessly from one set of exercises to the next. Finally, this exercise regimen should require no props or equipment, and be relatively fun (set to music?) and free. Any takers?

Chinese *Kung Fu*

This section will delve into the practice of Chinese *kung fu*, focusing primarily on the practice of *taiji quan*, as any discussion on *qigong* would be incomplete without doing so. In examining Chinese *kung fu*, it is important for us to differentiate it from other forms of martial arts of our world. For example, to strap a revolver around your waist, draw it and shoot is a form of martial art. The Western form of boxing, like that practised by Mohammad Ali, is also a form of martial art. The West too has its own differing forms of fencing and sword-fighting techniques. So, what is the difference between Western martial art and Chinese *kung fu*, if any? What is acceptable and what is unacceptable to the Christian, and why? One major difference is that Western martial arts are largely divorced from any religious or supernatural affiliations, their practice being anchored in the physical aspects of nifty footwork, balance, leverage and skill. Chinese *kung fu* incorporates many of the physical aspects of martial arts, but that is not all, because Chinese *kung fu* is not just about the physical movements of punching and kicking, etc.

Apart from the physical, Chinese *kung fu* is also about building up the internal strength, so that when a person punches, he is not simply exerting and throwing physical weight and strength into the punch, but he is also channelling *qi* into the punch to give it extra force. Breath control and *qi* are vital in the practice of Chinese *kung fu*. To help control their *qi* and to absorb more *qi* so as to grow in ability, those who practice Chinese *kung fu* are encouraged and taught Buddhist meditative techniques (to achieve a calm mind) and the breath control techniques of *qigong* (so as to better absorb and harness the *qi*). Many who join martial arts schools to learn

Chinese *kung fu* are often also required to pay regular homage to the founder of the school (ancestral worship) or a particular deity in the Chinese pantheon of gods (often *Guan Gong*, the god of war). We see in this that, though much of Chinese *kung fu* (and many Asian martial arts) is purely physical, it is hard to divorce it from the religious aspects of our Asian heritage and culture.

Taiji Quan

Taiji quan is a form of Chinese *kung fu* whose movements are derived from Daoist principles concerning the flow of the *Dao* in creation. In its practice, one is to flow with, rather than go against, the flow of nature as it is only when one is in harmony with nature that one is able to harness its energy for defence and offence. In the West, studies have been conducted into the benefits of *taiji quan* for the elderly. In a study conducted by Emory University in the US, it was found that those who practised *taiji* fell half as often as those who underwent traditional balance therapy. This and other studies have led the American Geriatric Association to view *taiji* as a favourable influence on the two important physical fitness traits of balance and strength (*AGA Journal*, May 1996). The article went to say that, unlike traditional therapies that require expensive electronic equipment, *taiji* exercises based on slow, controlled movements do not require much cost. From the studies conducted, it would appear that there are some real physical benefits to be derived from *taiji quan*.

Biblical Approach: It must be acknowledged that there are physical benefits to be gained from a practice of *taiji quan*. The slow movements do serve to loosen and keep the joints limber, as well as help a practitioner (particularly the elderly) gain and maintain a good sense of balance. Apart from the fact that it is an acclaimed cultural heritage of the Chinese, the systematic exercise regimen is a draw in and of itself. For believers, however, the decision on whether or not to engage in *taiji quan* may not rest purely on it being of some physical health value, or a systematic and appealing exercise regimen. We must consider the fact that in order for us to get the best out of this practice, we have to buy into and accept the religious philosophy that undergirds it. This is something believers cannot do.

Why Practise Chinese *Kung Fu*?

Ask most people why they engage in Chinese *kung fu* and you are more likely than not to get the answer that it is a good exercise regimen that promotes health. For some, this exercise regimen may turn itself into a sport (the national and international *wushu* or martial arts competitions). It must be mentioned that there is a growing worldwide appeal towards learning Chinese *kung fu* (which some view as an art form) because of the publicity it has received in movies. Few outside of the military (where lessons in some form or other of martial art is required) today would answer that they took up Chinese *kung fu* for self-defence, though I am sure that some do.

Biblical Approach: In our response to the practice of Chinese *kung fu*, we must first acknowledge that our primary concern is with the religious practices associated with much of it (for example, the channelling of *qi* and ancestral worship practices). The Bible is clear that we are to have nothing to do with these religious beliefs and practices (1 Corinthians 10:21). Acknowledging this as our primary concern frees us from the question of whether or not military personnel — like many young Singaporean men who have to undergo national service in the armed forces — may engage in the required martial art lessons. Believers who are military personnel may, in this case, take up the required lessons without fear of falling under spiritual oppression through associated religious practices, as these practices are not commonly carried out in secular armed forces.

Nonetheless, there is another concern and danger that we should be wary of, and that is with regard to our developing a propensity for violence. Our enemy is a crafty foe, and if he cannot capture us through the religious practices associated with Chinese *kung fu*, he will try to raise within us self-confidence and pride in our ability to defend ourselves, an obsession towards the art, and an inclination towards violence. We must guard against this. So, we would advise those who look to Chinese *kung fu* as a form of exercise or art form that there are many other equally good exercise regimens for them to engage in.

It is important for us to recognize that there is spiritual activity involved in many Asian martial arts and, with this realization, steer clear of all such practices. Ask yourself if it is worth putting your faith on the line when there are so many other forms of exercise regimens available, for example, swimming, walking, jogging, cycling and Pilates. In actual fact, the best way of staying healthy is to exercise by doing simple everyday things like climbing the stairs, walking from point to point, and eating healthily. The best forms of exercise are the things that we do on a daily basis for the whole day and not just for an hour or so a day.

Appendices

APPENDIX A

LONG, THE CHINESE DRAGON

The *long* (Chinese dragon) is a mythical creature that has come under the condemnation and ban of many Christians. I believe there are three basic reasons for this. First, is the veneration accorded to the *long* by the Chinese. Second, is the linking of the *long* to the dragon of Revelation 12, which has resulted in the *long* being viewed as a type or symbol of the devil. Third, is a fear that the possession of any item inscribed with an image of the *long* would lead to a right of entry being given to the evil spirits believed to be residing in or attached to that particular item.

Definition and Background: The dragon is a mythical creature, references to which may be found in both the Bible and the mythologies of the East and West. The term "dragon" is gleaned from the Greek word *drakon* and the Latin word *draco* or *draconis*. The Greek word, meaning "serpents", may be used to refer to either real or mythical snakes, or to snake-like figures. The Latin word may also be used to refer to actual serpents. Common usage today view dragons as mythical creatures "shaped like serpents or with serpent features, and often endowed with features or parts belonging to various animals".[1] The *long* is often described as having the head of a camel and the horns of a deer, with the eyes of a rabbit and the ears of a cow. In addition, it is also said to possess the neck of a snake, the belly of a frog, the scales of a carp (as a ridge along its back), the palms of a tiger, and the legs and claws of a hawk.[2] From the earliest times, the form attributed to the dragon has been many and varied. Nonetheless, regardless of its later forms, the dragon of mythology continues to remain essentially a serpent.

Belief in the myth of the dragon is both ancient and widespread; the most ancient traditions appear to date back to the Sumerian, Akkadian and Egyptian mythologies of the first three millennia BC. Within these ancient contexts, dragons represented forces or elements which interfered with the correct order and functioning of the world. In the Middle Eastern context, within which the Bible is written, the dragon symbolized great evil. It was, therefore, chosen and used in the Bible (the Revelation of John) when a word-picture or image of the devil[3] was required. The tradition of viewing dragons as destructive beings, responsible for death and disorder, has its roots in the ancient mythologies of the Near East, and of the Indian, Iranian and European world. This tradition is upheld by cultures located in the western regions of Eurasia and in some parts of East Africa. It has also continued "into the Christian culture of the European Middle Ages as well as into the Christian mythologies of Egypt and Ethiopia".[4] To the people of the Middle Eastern world, the serpent or dragon is symbolic of the principle of evil.[5]

The basic premise of the tradition — that dragons represent all that is chaotic, destructive and evil — is one reason why many Christians today destroy images of the dragon. However, this approach fails to take into account a second tradition, typical of East Asia (especially China, Indonesia and Japan), which represents dragons as powerful and helpful beings. To the Chinese, for example, the *long* is neither malicious nor poisonous like the Western dragon. Instead, it is generally viewed as a benevolent creature, most commonly associated with the outpouring of rain.[6] The attempt, however, to make a clear-cut distinction between the Western and Eastern concepts of dragons, as being evil and good respectively, is not always possible. That is because one may also find examples of benevolent dragons within the Eurasian mythological tradition, just as destructive dragons may be found in the mythological traditions associated with the East Asian dragon.

General Evaluation: The image of the *long* is viewed by some Christians to be an idolatrous image, infused with the demonic.[7] These people have drawn upon Revelation chapter 12 to speak against the use of the image of the *long*, in the belief that it is synonymous with the dragon mentioned in Revelation.[8] Calling on this biblical passage, some contend that images of the *long* must be condemned as idolatrous and destroyed because the Greek word *drakon* (from which the English word "dragon" is derived) means "serpent". This contention rests primarily on the use of the word "dragon" in the Bible and the English language reference of the *long* as a "dragon". Another proof text drawn upon to support this contention is that of the devil appearing to Eve in the form of a serpent in the Garden of Eden (Genesis 3). This, however, is too simplistic an argument that does not take into account the differing cultural interpretations and notions of the dragon, as well as the symbolic and, at times, differing uses applied to various images in the Bible.[9] Others advocate the view that while the dragon in the book of Revelation is not a direct reference to the *long*, the two dragons are similar in that both personify evil.

This view fails to take into account the fact that the *long* in Chinese mythology — considered partly a preserver and partly a destroyer[10] — is generally believed to be a benevolent creature venerated as a guardian of treasures and a symbol of authority, justice, and strength.[11] The belief in the *long*[12] grew out of the ancient Chinese belief in both good and evil spirits that could take on the physical forms of living beings such as apes, tigers, dogs and serpents of all varieties. As this belief grew and spread, the Chinese began to look upon disturbances in nature, natural disasters, sudden death and even insanity as the times when these spirits took authority over human lives and acted. To combat and counter the negative influence of the malevolent spirits, the Chinese turned to and began developing their pantheon of good spirits and gods. As a symbol of ancient China, the *long* is venerated as a harbinger of blessings and enjoys great significance within the ancient Chinese culture.[13] As the *long*, unlike the biblical and Western concept of the dragon, is deemed to be generally benevolent, it is really a little too simplistic for us to link the two images on the grounds that the image of a dragon represents evil.

The current trend advocates the belief that there are demonic spirits residing in or physically attached to the pantheon of inanimate idolatrous images, like the *long*. This belief is totally contrary to the teaching of the Bible (Psalm 115:4-8; Isaiah 44:12-20). There is, and can be, no demonic spirit residing in or attached to any material representation of the *long*. To advocate the possibility of a physical demonic possession of an inanimate material object with an imprint of the dragon would, as Dr Simon Chan expressed it, simply "pander to the devil's pride by exaggerating his malevolence"[14] and bring the Christian advocating such a belief under the control of the devil through the generation of superstitious fear. As believers, we must not allow the animistic beliefs of our culture to corrupt and cause our faith to degenerate into a form of Christian superstition. Doing so would merely glorify the devil and deny the victory purchased for us by Christ on the cross. Without underestimating the enemy, we must help Christians to be more aware and assured of their victory in Christ (over the devil). The devil is ultimately subservient to God, the sovereign ruler over all creation.

There is no power or demon in the physical representation of the *long*. The Christian objection to the *long* does not lie in it being a mythical creature, word-picture of consummate evil or possible representation of the devil, or even in it having a demonic spirit attached. It lies in the veneration (bordering on or running into worship) accorded to it by individuals and the overwhelming trust placed upon its efficacy to protect and deliver one from evil. Venerating the *long* in such a manner draws worship away from our Lord Jesus Christ. Evil spirits working to achieve this then move in to consolidate their attack on our psyche and faith, in the hope of drawing us deeper and deeper into a belief in the efficacy of the *long*, and further away from the worship of our Lord Jesus Christ. Believers must beware this deception of the devil and not fall into the trap of fear. Many have fallen into this trap, resulting in their going all out to destroy anything and everything inscribed with an image of a *long*.

Biblical Approach: How then are we to treat the *long* and its material representations? To begin with, let us be clear that the *long* is no more demonic than a chair on which we may sit. It is only when we start imputing to the image great power (through our worship and faith) that it takes on demonic dimensions. There is nothing about this image that we need fear. Did not Paul say that we are more than conquerors through Christ who loved us (Romans 8:37)? Any possible demonic influence is superseded by the fact that the earth and its fullness belong to the Lord (1 Corinthians 10:26). Paul also clearly teaches in 1 Corinthians 10:23-31 that we are not to be bound by the superstitious fear that the physical possession of any item linked with pagan worship would result in some form of spiritual oppression or possession. If this fear is real, Christians would not be able to keep in their possession any Singapore 50-dollar note because printed on it is the motif of a *long*. To believe anything other than what the Bible teaches us would undermine our Christian assurance of salvation and deny the victory that Christ has wrought for us on the cross at Calvary.

If we choose not to possess an image of the *long*, let it first be done for the sake of pleasing God (keeping our homes free from images of any pagan deities and spirits). Next, let it be done to break away from past bondages (renunciation of a belief in the efficacy of the *long* by having an image of it moulded onto the roof of our homes, or the obsessive collection of the image). Also, let it be done so that we would not stumble our "weaker" brethren who may yet believe that there are spirits attached to the image (the teaching received from former pagan beliefs or the erroneous teaching of certain Christians). In all this, it is important that we avoid the dual extremes of thinking either that there are demons in the image of the *long*, or that there is no spiritual activity whatsoever connected to the image. As it is a deity of the Chinese pantheon of spirit beings, spiritual activity is connected to the image of the *long*. The spiritual activity, however, is not within the image per se, but is linked to any active belief in either the efficacy of the *long* to guard and protect (held by the Chinese), or the presence of demons in any representative image of the *long* (held by Christians).

In conclusion, it must be reiterated that the belief that the *long* and the dragon of Revelation are synonymous stems from a hermeneutically wrong understanding of the Revelation text. It is not the intent of this passage of the Bible to present us with such a link. Nevertheless, believers must still treat the *long* with prejudice, because belief in the legends and myths associated with it has developed to the extent that it is viewed and revered as a deity with awesome powers. This is illustrated, for example, by the fact that no *Chun Jie* celebration would be complete without a Chinese dragon *(long)* dance to drive away evil spirits and usher in blessings.[15] The *long* must, therefore, be viewed and treated as any other idol or idolatrous image, but it does not deserve greater attention from believers than that given to any other idol. (For a discussion on how we are to deal with idols and idolatrous images, see Appendix D.)

Appendix B
An Attempt at Christianizing

In the course of Christian history, a number of pagan festivals have been christianized and assimilated into the Christian faith and practice, for example, Easter, which was originally a pagan harvest festival celebrating the arrival of spring. May we therefore consider christianizing any of the Chinese religious festivals? Let us examine the practice of certain Chinese Christians (both in Singapore and Malaysia) who, to this day, observe *Qing Ming Jie*. This observation of *Qing Ming Jie* is neither condoned nor condemned by their churches, as it is simply a practice that has been traditionally allowed to continue. During this festival, family members would visit the tomb of their ancestors (on the day *Qing Ming Jie* is celebrated), clean the tomb, light a couple of candles and make a bow (of respect to their ancestors). There have also been cases of certain nominal Christians (in Malaysia) burning "hell notes" (paper money) as an offering to their ancestors. It is held that the advantage of this continued observance, apart from the remembrance of our ancestors, lies in the Christian witness of our continued love and care for our dearly departed.

Note that for this witness to be effective we must be recognized as Christians when visiting the tomb; and our visit to the tomb must be witnessed or acknowledged by non-Christians. Our witness, in this case, is directed primarily towards our non-Christian relatives and friends. This being the case, our daily Christian witness is as important, if not more so, as that of an annual visit to the tomb during *Qing Ming Jie*. It is necessary for Christians to show love and concern for their relatives and friends while they are yet alive, and not simply remember them once a year after they have passed away. While some view *Qing Ming Jie* as an opportunity for Christians to witness to their non-Christian relatives and friends, others consider it disadvantageous for these reasons:

1. The potential corruption of our Christian faith and erosion of the authority of the Bible should Christians lapse into the traditional ideas and practice of ancestral worship (for example, those mentioned earlier who burn "hell notes" to the dead);
2. The tendency for the initial concepts behind any attempts at christianizing to become either eroded or corrupted in time;
3. The possible stumbling of fellow Christians (1 Corinthians 8:7-13) who view such an attempt at christianizing as leading to a compromise of our faith;
4. The lack of a clear break from the past for converts, especially the elderly (in whom religious and ancestral worship practices have become ingrained).

Of course, it may be said of the last point that attempts at christianizing could also serve as a means by which converts may be "eased" into the Christian faith, without having to experience too drastic a "loss" of our traditional Chinese heritage. The question, however, would then arise with regard to when a total break would or should come about, as well as the areas and things from which we must immediately separate ourselves and those we may ease into. In theory, Christians may observe *Qing Ming Jie*, so long as we have a clear understanding of and uphold the following:

1. A clear Christian perspective of the scale of veneration (see Appendix C);
2. A clear understanding and observance of what may and what may not be done in the keeping of *Qing Ming Jie;*
3. The need to establish a balance between witnessing to non-believers of our continued Christian love for the departed, and avoidance of becoming a stumbling block to new converts and our "weaker brethren" (1 Corinthians 8:7-13).

In actual practice, however, the christianizing of this festival is not so clear-cut. To implement the three points stated above, clear teaching is required, as well as firm pastoral oversight and where necessary, discipline. This is important because *Qing Ming Jie* (unlike Easter) is still a very real part of a living religion. We are not, therefore, able to wholly take over this festival to give its observance a Christian basis. There is a constant danger of our Christian faith being corrupted. We must acknowledge that the danger of a corruption of our faith exists even in our Christian celebration of All Souls' Day, when Christians traditionally commemorate the passing of their loved ones.

An example of this may be gleaned from an article published in the 2 November 1992 issue of *The Straits Times* that highlighted the Philippine celebration of All Souls' Day on 1 November 1992. The observation made was that, "Many spent Saturday night in the cemeteries to beat yesterday's rush, some holding impromptu karaoke sing-a-long sessions amid the gravestones." On All Souls' Day itself, the article noted, "People carrying flowers, candles, food and cassette players headed for the cemeteries in droves, while entrepreneurs leaned ladders up against the concrete cemetery walls and charged visitors one peso each to circumvent the mob at the main entrance. Others sold ceremonial candles or food ranging from fresh fruit to simmering pigs' innards." In addition, it was also observed that, "Tombs were converted into feast tables, flowers gave way to playing cards and dice, sorrow turned to laughter and the blare of pop music as mourners celebrated one of the impoverished country's biggest festival of the year."

Thus we learn that any festival, be it Christian or not, run the risk of being corrupted. In most cases, however, the festivals themselves are doctrinally neutral.[1] The factor we need examine, therefore, is the intent of the celebrant and participants. For example, what is the intent behind the lighting of candles? Are we engaging in the veneration or worship of the dead? The question of intent is a very difficult one to settle. A major difficulty lies in that while one may intellectually hold to a spiritually sound basis for the celebration of these festivals (for example, a commemoration of the dead), the actions often belie a different belief (for example, in the efficacy of the dead to bless and curse). What then may or may not be done for a Christian observance of *Qing Ming Jie*?

To begin, the cleaning of the tomb is quite an acceptable practice and should be observed. One should, however, be careful about lighting two candles before the tomb, due to the connotation of setting up an altar (to the deceased) associated with this act. That which clearly must never be done is the offering of "hell notes", incense and food, etc. The principle established in 1 Corinthians 8:7-13 must dictate whether or not the act of bowing to the deceased may be observed. It may also be applied to any other acts associated with the practice of ancestral veneration. We have been granted a certain Christian freedom in Jesus Christ (Galatians 5:1) but this freedom is to be tempered with Christian responsibility and love (Galatians 5:13ff; 1 Peter 2:16). Therefore, before participating in activities such as *Qing Ming Jie* based on one's Christian freedom to do so, consider if this act would a) please God (Exodus 20:1-7; 1 Corinthians 10); and b) stumble our "weaker brethren" (1 Corinthians 8:7-13; 10:24). We must not engage in acts simply to express our Christian freedom and bring fulfilment to ourselves. Rather, all that we do must be done for the glory of God and the establishment of His kingdom here on earth (1 Corinthians 6:20b; Philippians 1:20).

Appendix C
The Scale of Veneration

In the Christian perspective of the Scale of Veneration, a clear distinction is made between the worship of God and the practices of respect for living elders, veneration of the deceased, and the worship of idols and the devil (the Bible teaches against and condemns these last two practices). There is no such distinction in the animistic perspective, where the lines between each aspect of the Scale of Veneration are blurred.

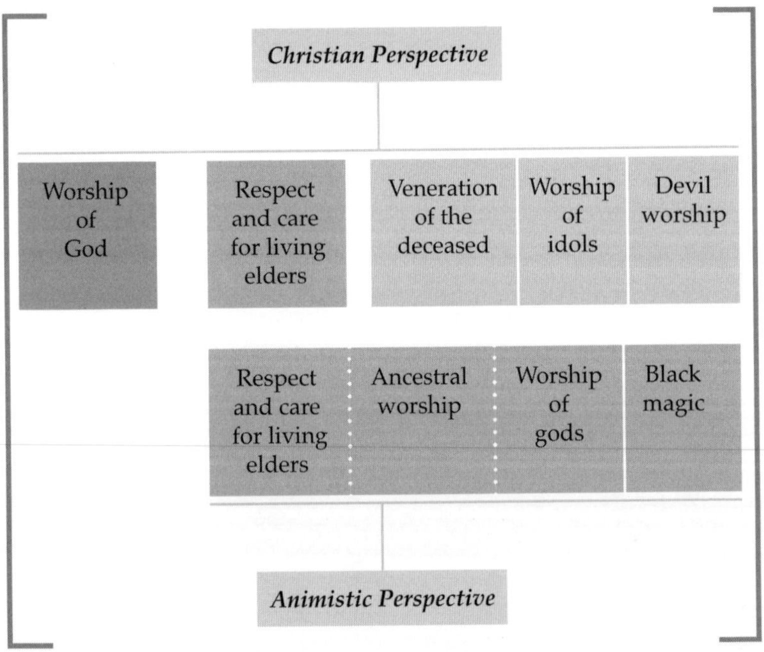

In the latter perspective, one's practice of respect for living elders may easily slip into the practice of ancestral worship (as one seeks the blessings, guidance and protection of one's departed). The worship of false gods lies not too far away as the next step along the Scale (as our ancestors achieve immortality). From there one may easily enter into the practice of various rituals and rites cum black magic (as we seek to control the spirits in order to achieve our own desires).[1]

Appendix D
Images of Worship

The ancestral tablet is believed to be the residence of one of the three souls of a deceased. With this in mind, how are we as believers to view the ancestral tablet? In general, many believers look upon the ancestral tablet as an idol, but what do they mean by this? Yes, many of us regard religious figurines, like those of *Guan Yin* or Buddha, as idols, but do we know what actually makes them so? Before we answer this, let us turn our attention to another belief concerning idols. Many Christians believe that there are evil spirits present in idols. Is this really true? Note the similarity of this idea to the Chinese belief that the ancestral tablet is the residence of one soul of a deceased. Now ask yourself, is the perception that demons reside in idols a belief drawn from the Bible or one drawn from traditional Chinese belief? It is important for us to understand the influence of evil spirits over an idol, as it will determine how we view and treat an idol, and everything associated with it.

Deuteronomy 4:28, Psalm 115:4-8 and Isaiah 44:12-20 clearly state that idols are nothing, the mere work of man that have neither life nor power. To say that idols have life and power is to place oneself in a rather awkward position because if I, for example, carve an idol, then I am by right its creator. As its creator, I should be more powerful than the idol. Yet, instead of exerting my authority, I choose to bow down to it, thereby making the created thing lord and master over me, its very own creator. What a ridiculous situation this would be. Alternatively, one might argue that an idol that has just been made has no demonic presence, life or power within it. If this is the case, we must ask a couple of other questions. First, when does a newly made idol gain the presence of an evil spirit and along with it, spiritual life and power? Second, how then are we to treat these freshly made or mass-produced idols? Are they still idols in the first place? Many would be hard-pressed to find logical answers to these questions because, in essence, they are still operating on the mindset that evil spirits reside in idols.

The idea that demons reside in idols gives us cause for alarm, and indeed many have gone about destroying idols for fear that if they did not, the spirits within would somehow cause them harm. In such a scenario, what is a believer to do if he is living in a home full of idols? He cannot go around destroying these idols, as they do not belong to him. Yet, the concern and fear is that evil spirits reside in every one of them. What is this person to do? Note that this thinking is not in line with the teaching of the Bible and serves only to give the wrong impression that the devil is very powerful, while our God and we, the children of God, are weak. The teaching that evil spirits reside in idols is an animistic perspective not supported or encouraged by the Bible, which holds clearly to the perspective that idols are nothing but the work of our own hands. Understanding this frees us from the fear of being confronted with and attacked by demons every time we encounter an idol.

The Bible teaches that when people make offerings to idols, they are, in fact, making offerings to the demon / s *behind* the idol (1 Corinthians 10:20). That is to say, the image of the idol serves merely as camouflage to deceive a person into worshipping the devil, something most would not voluntarily do. For example, should the devil appear before us in a red jumpsuit, with horns, a tail and pitchfork in hand (a traditional Western projection of the devil), not many would want to follow after and worship him. Should he, on the other hand, appear as a sweet and gentle lady or a wise and benevolent old man, or any other image pleasing to our sight and reassuring to our mind, the outcome would be quite different. Yet, these are but the external disguises of the devil. When a person is caught up in the worship of the devil in this way, these disguises become for that person an idol, as he sells his "soul" in worship to the devil. Which brings us to the point that it is precisely our worship that the devil is after and if we understand this, we will understand that demons are not present in idols but in the hearts and lives of all who bow down in worship to these idols. Idols are nothing. The focus of our worship is everything.

Getting back to a question we asked earlier, the answer is that it is our worship that makes a figurine efficacious, not the thought that there is an evil spirit resident within the figurine or ancestral tablet. Now that this has been established, what is our next step? What are we to do with these idolatrous items? Well, we must be careful not to seek to remove idols from our midst out of fear because there is nothing to fear about them, and to fear is to fall into the trap of the enemy as we turn our eyes of faith away from our sovereign Lord to believe the enemy's lie. Nonetheless, the Bible does advocate the removal and destruction of idols from our midst for the following reasons: To begin with, it is to be carried out by those who have held a belief in the power of these idols, as an act of renunciation and cleansing of ourselves from the mindsets and habits of our idolatrous past (1 Corinthians 8:7; Ephesians 4:17-24). Next, we are to do so, that we may prove a good witness to non-Christians and to all who turn to Christ, who may be similarly challenged to remove idolatrous items in their possession (1 Corinthians 8:7-13).

For example, what sort of a witness can I be if I encourage a person who has recently accepted Christ to make a clean break from his past by removing idolatrous items in his possession, and yet keep similar items in my home as a work of art? In this instance, I would definitely stumble my brethren. The most important reason for removing idolatrous items, however, is our innate desire to obey God and please Him (John 8:29; 1 John 3:18-22). Our Lord is a jealous God and He has commanded that we are not to make for ourselves "an idol or any likeness of what is in heaven above or on the earth beneath or in the water under the earth" (Exodus 20:4). Some may find the idea that God could be jealous to be beneath Him as God. Let us understand that His jealousy stems from love and the desire to see one and all saved. The command must, therefore, be understood in relation to His desire to protect us from the devil and not simply the result of selfish desire.

All of us can understand this form of jealousy. For example, should you get married, would you still hang prominently on a wall in your new home the photographs of all your old dates? Would you like it if your spouse hung up on the wall the photographs of all his or her old dates? If you would not like that to be done to you and would not do it to your spouse, why should

God be treated any differently and less? As children of God, let us return love to Him by willingly and ungrudgingly removing all idolatrous items from our midst, regardless of the financial (the jade or gold content), aesthetic (the beautiful and intricate craftsmanship) or emotional (the ancestral tablets of our ancestors) cost. The Bible is clear that we are not to covet that by which idols and idolatrous items are made (Deuteronomy 4:15-19; 1 Chronicles 14:12). All are to be crushed, burned and utterly destroyed, and removed from our midst. Our faith and relationship with God must take precedence over all.

Appendix E

Food Offered to Idols

Is it permissible for believers to eat food that has been offered to idols? Would anything (good or bad) happen to us if we did? These are questions constantly and commonly asked by Christians in places where it is a common practice for people to make offerings of food to idols. The answer generally given to these questions is that we should not eat such food, lest the devil is given a "legal right of entry" into our lives. However, the call to abstain from eating such food is easier said than done. This is especially so in Asia, where the food we buy from the market and consume in food courts are often sold to us by those actively engaged in the worship of idols. The food served in many homes too would have first been offered to an idol or an ancestor. Even the Western-influenced fast-food restaurants are not exempt, as most now serve meat slaughtered according to certain religious guidelines. What then are we to do?

Some, including many who believe that eating food offered to idols could provide the enemy with a doorway into our lives, have attempted to get around this issue by applying 1 Corinthians 10:25 and 27 where we are taught: "Eat anything that is sold in the meat market, without asking questions for conscience's sake…If one of the unbelievers invites you, and you want to go, eat anything that is set before you, without asking questions for conscience's sake." What do these people mean? Are they saying that if we eat anything with full knowledge of it having been offered to an idol, we are open to spiritual attack, but if we are ignorant of the fact, then we are safe? This cannot be correct. If partaking of food that has been offered to idols exposes us to spiritual attack, then this would be the case regardless of our knowledge or ignorance. The evil spirits will not bother with semantics, or with our awareness or unawareness of the facts. 1 Corinthians 10:25 and 27 are not to be understood in this way.

The Bible teaches us that an idol is lifeless, the mere moulding of earthly materials by human hands (Psalm 115:4-8). If lifeless, then they are also powerless; and if powerless, what effect can they have over any food placed before them (1 Corinthians 8:4)? Even if we accept the possibility that idols have power, the Bible assures us that we need not fear because "yet for us there is but one God, the Father, from whom are all things and we exist for Him; and one Lord, Jesus Christ, by whom are all things, and we exist through Him" (1 Corinthians 8:6). The Bible is clear in proclaiming that as children of God, we need have no fear that partaking of such food could harm us or lead to us being spiritually attacked (Mark 16:17,18; Luke 10:17-20; 1 Corinthians 8:4-6). A careful examination of the Bible would reveal that it clearly does not prohibit the consumption of food that has been offered to idols, in and of itself. The context, however, within which this food is consumed must be carefully examined and chosen — there are three primary contexts within which food that has been offered to idols is not to be eaten.

The first context is to be found in the life of a new convert. When one turns to Christ, it is important for one to renounce and set aside all past practices, performed in worship of an idol or in a belief in the efficacy of that idol. This is to allow time for the young believer to grow in faith and maturity, laying aside the fears and false beliefs of his past that may cause him to stumble in his current walk with God (1 Corinthians 8:7). The second context arises when our liberty in Christ may lead a fellow believer to stumble in his faith. Our knowledge of the sovereignty of God frees us to partake of food offered to idols without fear or belief in the efficacy of the act of sacrificing (food) to idols. A new convert or fellow believer may not have fully assimilated this knowledge into his life. Hence, on seeing us partake of the food, he may do so too, but with either a fear of being spiritually attacked or the mistaken idea that we are affirming the efficacy of the sacrificial offering. The Bible teaches us that this is to be avoided (1 Corinthians 8:9-13).

The final context that we are to avoid is that of our participation in feasts and ceremonies linked to the worship of idols. To participate in these ceremonies is to non-verbally affirm the efficacy of the idol. To partake of the food offered at such occasions is to share in the worship and declaration of allegiance to the spirits behind this false worship of idols (1 Corinthians 10: 18-22). This we must never do, as our worship and sacrifices of praise belong to Christ alone. This context is linked to our second context, in that we are not to stumble another believer by our bad witness or harm the witness of another believer. (For example, if we visit the family of a believer who has made a stand of not eating food that has been offered to idols, we should not eat such food as well.) Above all, Christians must learn in all things to do only that which is well pleasing to God (John 8:29; 1 John 3:18-22).

The fact that sacrifices made to idols are actually received by demons is clearly attested to in the Bible (Deuteronomy 32:

17; Psalm 106:37,38). This brings us back to the belief in the "legal right" of the devil to enter into our lives the moment we partake of food that has been offered to idols. As explained above, this is a mistaken belief. The entry of evil spirits into our lives cannot be gained through the mere consumption of food. If it could, most of us in Asia would now be spiritually oppressed or possessed, as it is nearly impossible for us to avoid eating food that has been offered to idols at least once. The devil gains entry into our lives through the worship we express, as we believe and participate in the idolatrous teachings and ceremonies around us. When we participate in idolatrous feasts, we share in the worship of the idol and the offering of sacrifices to the evil spirits behind it. This participation and worship then serve as an invitation for the enemy to enter our lives and rule over us. The "legal right" of entry for the enemy is derived from our worship of pagan idols and false deities, not the food we consume.

Related to the issue of eating food that has been offered to idols is the question concerning blood. Is it permissible for believers to eat blood? It is generally taught that one should refrain from eating blood and the Bible passages commonly used to support this position are Leviticus 17:14 and Acts 15:20. Many today, however, continue to ponder over this question, searching for a clear rationale for the call to abstain from eating blood. Is this rule applicable to us today? The instituting of the cultic practice (of not eating blood) as a formal rule may be traced back to the post-flood days of Noah (Genesis 9:4-7) where it served primarily as a declaration of the value of human life in the eyes of God.

"The statement about blood (verse 4)...Though it may originally have been a cultic rule, (it) now stands as part of a formidable barrier against dehumanization. An old statement on blood has now been transformed into an affirmation about human life and human worth. This decree urges human enhancement and the valuing of human persons. In this post-flood decree of creation, the sanctity of human life is established against every ideology and every force which would cheapen or diminish life."[1]

The prohibition in Genesis 9:4ff on the consumption of blood is a rule to be adhered to by all mankind. The Israelites were not specifically targeted here, as their rise and development as a specific race and nation did not take place till very much later. The great worth of a human life is recognized, hence the related injunction against the taking of human life (verse 5). Human life is to be valued and viewed as sacred because man is made in the image of God (verse 6).[2] The next time this rule is encountered, we find the Israelites in the wilderness receiving instruction from the Lord on the offering of sacrifices (Leviticus 7:26,27;17). For the Israelites then, animals were to be slaughtered only in the Tabernacle. One possible reason for this is the attempt to prevent the secret worship and offering of animal sacrifices to the goat-demons outside the camp. In the Tabernacle, the blood of the animal sacrifices was poured out to the Lord as an offering for the atonement of sins. The primary objective for the injunction against the consumption of blood in this case is the establishment of the use of blood as a means of atonement (Leviticus 17:11).

As it is to be used for the atonement of sins, the blood of animals should, therefore, be considered sacred by the Israelites. Hence, they should refrain from eating blood. Secondarily, the call to abstain from eating blood in Leviticus might have been directed towards those engaged in the worship of goat-demons. Blood sacrifices would have been part and parcel of such worship, as would the consumption of the offered blood by the worshippers. Thus, the injunction against the eating of blood "might have been directed, in part at least, against the superstition that by eating the blood in which is the life of the totem animal, the worshipper appropriated the life of the god".[3] There is no truth to this superstition and it is not to be adhered to. Any who were formerly or are currently engaged in such practices are to renounce and stop them, refraining from consuming blood to separate themselves from their idolatrous practices and beliefs. The third time this rule is encountered is "at the end of the Mosaic period and immediately prior to the entry of the Israelites into the promised land."[4] Up till this point, the Israelites could only slaughter animals they intended to eat in the Tabernacle. This was easily done as they were all camped around the Tabernacle.

The Israelites, however, were soon to cross over into and take possession of the promised land throughout which they would be scattered. New instruction had to be given to affirm that animals meant for food could be slaughtered, not just in the Tabernacle, but anywhere (Deuteronomy 12:15,20-22). However, one could only slaughter and offer animals as a sacrifice in certain designated places (Deuteronomy 12:10-14). It was also ruled that the blood of every slaughtered animal — be it for food or as sacrifice — was to be poured out to the Lord (Deuteronomy 12:16,27). The reason given is that "the blood is the life" (Deuteronomy 12:23-25). Blood is the sacred portion that belongs to God because it represents the life imparted to us by God, a life that only He may remove from existence. For the Israelites to eat blood, therefore, was to despise life. To refrain from eating blood is to honour and respect all life. To eat blood is to deny the sovereignty of God over all life, but to refrain from it is to acknowledge that all life rests in the hands of God.

Conclusion: In general, I would encourage believers living with those engaged in ancestral worship to avoid eating food offered to ancestors that is served during family meals, as a sign of our commitment to Christ and our separation from idolatrous worship. In addition, if some members abstain from taking such food, it is good for those in the family who later turn to Christ to follow and support their decision, so as to present the rest of the family with a consolidated witness. Many people (parents and elders), once they have come to terms with the change of faith and the stand on food, would set aside certain dishes that have not been offered to the ancestors, for Christian members of the family. The decision to abstain or not to abstain, however, rests totally with the conscience of each individual so none should try to judge another, whatever the decision taken.

The imagery of blood as life is not as strong in the modern world (except in various third-world nations) as it used to be when blood sacrifices and the slaughtering of animals for food were common everyday occurrences. Wars and murder, however, have remained a constant and very real part of all our lives, wherein blood is shed and lives are lost. This being the case, I believe that it is good and right for the injunction of the Bible to abstain from partaking of blood to be upheld. Christians should consciously decide to refrain from eating blood in any form, allowing this abstention to act as a constant reminder that we do not hold our own lives, and are not to attempt to hold the lives of others, in our hands. God is sovereignly in charge of all life and He alone has the right to give or take it away.

Appendix F

The Five Elements and Their Relationships

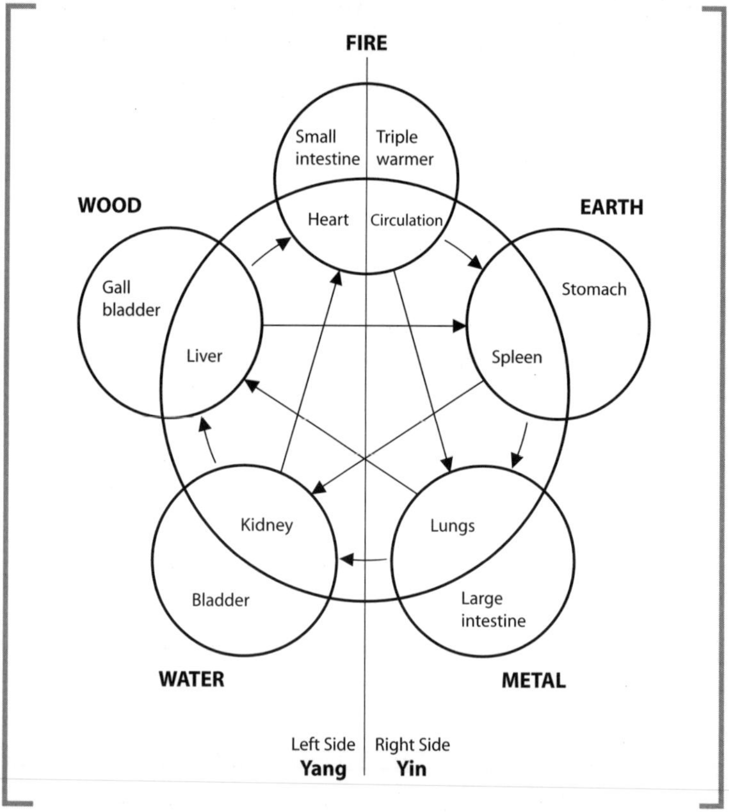

Outer Arrows:	"Creating" relationships
Inner Arrows (star pattern):	"Subjugating" relationships

* Taken from *New Age Medicine* by Paul C. Reisser, Teri K. Reisser and John Weldon. © 1987 Arthur Whitehead, Jr., Publisher. Used by permission of Dr John Weldon.

Appendix G

The 12 Meridians or *Jing Luo*

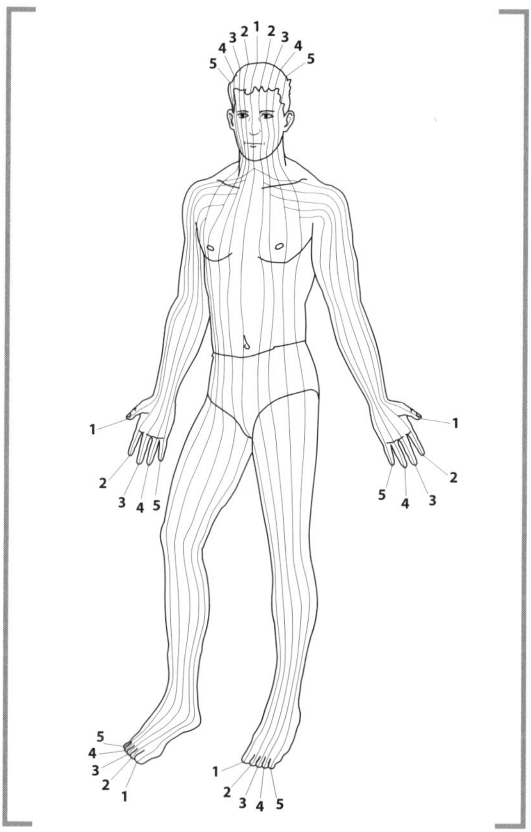

Each numbered line represents the CENTRE of its representative meridian on the body.

Appendix H

Handling Objections and Difficult Questions

This appendix, though not directly related to the matters discussed in this book, has been included to encourage those regularly faced with such matters and to provide some guidance on how they may be addressed.

Christianity and The West

Christianity Is a Western Religion

Yes, as a result of certain historical developments, Christianity did come to us from the West. As we would accept anything beneficial from the West, for example, refrigerators, air conditioners, physics, chemistry and computer technology, we would also do well to accept the truth to be found in the Christian faith. Besides, it is a known fact that Christianity actually originated in Asia, with 39 of the 40 authors of the Bible being Asian. The only author not from Asia is from Greece, in Europe. It would, therefore, be probably more correct to say that Christianity is not a Western, but an Asian religion.

Christianity and the Opium War

It is true that in history, Westerners who called themselves Christians were involved in oppressing the Chinese. We need to, however, learn to differentiate Western imperialism and the Opium War in China from Christianity. While it is true that Westerners did much harm, it must be acknowledged that there were also many good and well-meaning Western Christians who contributed greatly to China, such as in the establishment of various institutions, for example, hospitals, schools and universities, orphanages and homes for lepers and the aged.

Till Death Do Us Part?

Desire to Be With a Deceased Spouse

There are many who, though they have come to accept the truth of the Gospel of Christ, still cling on to their old ways because of their desire to be with their departed partner in the afterlife. Acknowledge the love shared and continued attachment of the living for the departed spouse, but raise the question and address the uncertainty of where the deceased may now be. If the deceased did not know Jesus, the Bible is clear that he faces eternal damnation. Bring across the point that in such a situation, the deceased would not want his living spouse to join him in suffering. This would only add to the suffering of the deceased. Cite the story of Lazarus and the rich man (Luke 16:19-31). Express your love and desire for your relative to join you in heaven. Bear testimony to your assurance of salvation (John 3:16).

Waiting for Spouse So As to Embrace Christianity Together

The ideal is for both husband and wife to become Christians (together). It is good at times to wait just a little longer, so as not to impose any sense of coercion on the unbelieving spouse. We should not, however, wait too long or both may lose the opportunity to accept Christ. The believing spouse should be encouraged to make a firm decision and become a committed and baptized member of a church. He may then set the example and continue to seek to influence his spouse to accept the truth of the Gospel of Christ.

Fear of Rejection and Punishment

Fear of Punishment and Calamity

Many who are steeped in idol worship are afraid to become Christians for fear that the deities they have been worshipping may get angry and cause them harm. Testimonies have also been received of how, upon the removal of idols from their homes, people started to experience greater calamities and mishaps. Many faced with such a situation have reclaimed and re-established these idols, causing them to become even more entrenched in their worship of idols. It must be recognized that this is precisely the ploy of the devil. The idols are nothing, but the enemy will attempt to lead people to believe that they have power, so as to lure these people back into a worship of the idols and the evil spirits behind them.

We must teach those who turn to Christ that our Lord Jesus Christ is God, Creator of the universe, and sovereignly able to protect and keep us from all harm. Christians must, however, be ready to stand firm against any backlash from the devil as a result of our rejection of him. This statement is not made out of a lack of faith in the ability of God, but simply as a statement of fact, because it could well be that our Lord wants us to be so tested. If we are, our response must be like that of Shadrach, Meshach and Abed-nego who, in the face of being thrown into the fiery furnace by Nebuchadnezzar, proclaimed that God was more than able to deliver them. Yet, should God choose not to, but allow them to continue to face the trial, these three men would not lose faith, but would continue to believe and trust in Him (Daniel 3:16-18).

Fear of Persecution and Rejection by Loved Ones

It is important that those who turn to Christ make known their faith to their family as soon as possible. The situation following this revelation may initially be very difficult as relatives come to terms with the fact or try to dissuade such a change in the believers' lives. Nonetheless, if we believe the Gospel to be the truth, we must persevere in our faith, as we then become a prime vehicle for bringing the Gospel to our family.

Filial Piety and Ancestral Worship

My Child Is Never at Home

A common complaint against Christians by parents is that they are so busy in church that they are hardly at home and have no time for the family. It is not right for Christians to be so involved in church or their own secular activities that they neglect their family relationships and responsibilities. A balance must be struck. Christians should exhibit their filial piety by helping their parents with household chores and, where appropriate and able, financially.

No One to Make Offerings

Many parents engaged in ancestral worship object to their children becoming Christians out of the concern that there will be no one to make offerings to them after they are dead and gone. It is true that believers are not to engage in such practices. The only thing we can do when faced with such a concern is to try to assure our parents of our love for them by ensuring that they are well provided for in this life. We should also share with them the Gospel of Christ and express our desire for them to receive Jesus Christ as their Lord and Saviour as we have, so we may be re-united as a family in heaven when our Lord Jesus returns to take us all home.

Believers Have No Sense of Filial Piety

This accusation is often levelled against believers because of our refusal to perform funeral rites and visit the tomb of our departed during *Qing Ming Jie*. Believers should not aggravate the issue by trying to argue the point, for example, on whether our parents prefer us to be filial towards them while they are alive or after they have passed away. Our only true defence and testimony is to ensure that we express filial piety towards our parents daily, in big and small ways. Note, too, that in Christianity, filial piety towards the deceased is expressed through *bi-annual* visits to the tomb/s (during Easter in April and on All Souls' Day in November), and *annual* memorial services (during Easter).

Living Moral Lives

All Religions Teach Us to Lead Morally Good Lives

Teachings on the living of good moral lives may be respected, irrespective of the religion propagating it. However, it must be communicated that good deeds and a good life cannot gain or assure us of a place in heaven (Ephesians 2:8,9) because no one can ever walk through this life without sinning. Jesus Christ, by His work on the cross, is the only one able to give the assurance that all who believe and receive Him as Lord and Saviour, would be forgiven their sins and saved (John 10:27,28; 14:6).

Many Christians Lie, Cheat and Throw Tantrums

Yes, this is true. Christians continue to have shortcomings, weaknesses and the propensity to make mistakes and hurt people. This is because, though redeemed and saved from our sins, we are not yet perfect. We are, however, on the road to perfection (sanctification) in Christ (Hebrews 12). We must encourage those disgusted by these failures in Christians to place their trust in Jesus Christ and not in His human followers (Christians). The failure of Christians to follow in the likeness of Christ must not be equated to the inability of Christ to redeem and save us. The shortcomings of Christians simply emphasize our need for Christ and go to show the great love of Christ, who died and rose again for us while we were yet sinners (Romans 5:6-11). We need not be perfect before accepting Christ.

I Live a Good Life and Perform Many Charitable Deeds

Many do not see the need to accept Jesus Christ into their lives, believing that they are good people not bound by sin as some others are. To these people, it must be communicated that it is good to be confident, but we must realize our personal limitations. Take children, for example. We look upon them as pure and innocent. Yet, without the necessity of any input on our part, many grow up learning to manipulate their elders with their tears and loud tantrums. As they grow, they also learn to tell lies and fight. It is impossible to live a totally sinless life (Romans 3:23,24), just as it is impossible to try to work our way to heaven by our own strength (John 14:6). We need Jesus!

End Notes

Laying the Foundation

1. For a fuller description, see Scott W. Sunquist (ed.); *A Dictionary of Asian Christianity;* Grand Rapids, Michigan: William B. Eerdmans Publishing Company; 2001; page 200.
2. "*Hanuman* the monkey king is the son of *Vayu*, the Hindu god of wind, and is looked upon by Hindus as the ultimate hero. He represents the figure of the ideal being as he is humble yet brave. His physical prowess, mental discipline and spiritual purity have made him extremely popular all over India." Extract from the website: www.siamese-dream.com/reference/hanuman.html
3. Colloquial Singapore English.
4. The recognition of the pagan gods as demons arose out of the awareness that these gods "did in fact have supernatural powers. Since there was only one God, such power could not be attributed to a god; hence the belief arose that idols represented demonic spirits." Gordon Fee; *The First Epistle to the Corinthians*; NICNT; Grand Rapids, Michigan:

William B. Eerdmans Publishing Company; Reprinted November 1988; page 472.

The Main Events

1. For example, most Chinese families like to hang the Chinese character *"fu"*, meaning blessing, upside down in their homes to symbolize blessing coming upon the family.
2. The Chinese Spiritual Warfare Network Initiative in Singapore did promote a celebration of *Zhong Qiu Jie*. As they explained, the fullness of the moon serves as a reminder that one must:
    - praise and glorify our God who created the moon, sun, stars and our planet earth in all their splendour; and
    - proclaim our belief that our lives (like the fully rounded moon) have been made complete by the grace, mercy and love of God, through faith in Jesus Christ.
3. *The Sunday Times,* 25 October 1998.
4. See Figure 5 in Chapter 6, Point 4 in the left-hand column.

Ancestral Veneration

1. Bong Rin Ro (ed.); *Christian Alternatives to Ancestor Practices;* Taiwan: Asian Theological Association; 1985; pages 123,124.
2. In general, the basic roots of ancestral worship may be traced back to the practice of totemism. Dr *Wei Yuan-Kwei* advocates totemism to be "the belief in and worship of an animate or inanimate object that is supposed to have an intimate relationship with an individual or a group". Bong

Rin Ro (ed.); ibid.; page 120.

3. "When Death Is Not Their Last Goodbye"; *The Straits Times;* Singapore: Singapore Press Holdings; 4 October 1996.
4. David A. Brown; *A Guide to Religions;* England: SPCK; 1987; page 129.
5. Certain Buddhist cults claim that they have a secret phrase that encompasses the whole of their divine revelation. In speaking this phrase repeatedly in their meditations, practitioners believe they are both proclaiming and allowing that divine revelation to permeate their whole being. As a result of this, it is believed that one may attain enlightenment and immortality.
6. Paul Enns; *The Moody Handbook of Theology;* Chicago: Moody Press; 1989; pages 372-374.
7. See Paul Enns; ibid.; pages 374-375 for a more detailed discussion of *Sheol* and *Hades*.
8. It is interesting to note that the medieval Christian church perceived hell to be a place of fire, where one of the judgements that people will face for their crimes requires the guilty to be boiled in oil. A similar belief may be found in Chinese mythology.
9. R. Pierce Beaver (con. ed., et. al.); *The World's Religions;* England: Lion's Publishing plc; First paperback edition, 1988; page 247.
10. While all agree that the body forms one part of the total make-up of human beings, there are two opposing views with regard to the "soul" and the "spirit" mentioned in the Bible, being the other parts of a human being. Those who hold that human beings are composed of two parts, view the "soul" and "spirit" to be the same substance, exercising

different functions. Others maintain the "soul" and "spirit" to be different both in substance and function, thus giving rise to the idea that human beings are composed of three parts. For a fuller discussion of this issue, see Paul Enns; op. cit.; pages 304-307.

11. Both the Bible and Christian tradition are rather ambiguous with regard to where a believer will be interred upon death, and after the final judgement and resurrection. For a fuller discussion of the intermediate state, see Sinclair B. Ferguson and David F. Wright (eds.); *New Dictionary of Theology;* Leicester, England: Inter-Varsity Press; Reprinted, 1989; pages 230 and 339-340.

12. William McDougall advocates that almost every existing race of human beings, no matter how lowly their grade of culture, or how limited their mental powers, generally hold to the belief that a person consists of both a physical and a "shadowy vapour-like duplicate of his body". The latter is deemed to be able to leave the body and transport itself rapidly from place to place; manifesting in those places all or most of the powers that are exerted in the physical body during one's "waking-life". These shadowy duplicates or ghost-souls are believed to be anthropomorphic in nature, having many of the properties of matter and the same needs as the embodied soul. They are, therefore, subject to hunger and thirst, the pains of cold and heat, and to a certain extent, the limitations of space and matter. William McDougall; *Body and Mind;* London: Metheun Publishers; Eighth Edition, 1938.

13. David Burnett; *Clash of Worlds;* Eastbourne: Monarch Publications Ltd; 1990; pages 93-95.

14. Leong Heng Keng (chairman, Committee on Chinese

Customs and Rites); *Chinese Customs and Festivals;* Singapore: Singapore Federation of Chinese Clan Associations; 1989; page 94.

15. These days, Buddhists have also started performing rites for the dead — in the meditation of the sutras, etc. This is not strictly a Buddhist practice, but an incorporation of the ideas of Daoism and ancestral worship into the Buddhist mindset.
16. It is not possible to adhere to this practice in Singapore because a government body assigns all burial plots.
17. A strand of Chinese superstitious belief advocates that one must be buried with all of one's body parts, or else one would be incomplete in the nether world. Many in the past, therefore, did not accept the practice of cremation, as it meant destroying the physical body. However, due to land shortage in Singapore, the practice of cremation is now quite well accepted. The ashes of the deceased would then be placed in a temple or columbarium, or on the family altar in the home. As Christians, there is no need for us to fear being buried without any part of our physical body or of being cremated, as we shall be given a "new body" when we are resurrected with Christ on the Last Day (1 Corinthians 15:43-53; Philippians 3:20,21).
18. We have the Christian freedom to partake of these without fear of falling into any demonic bondage, but this freedom must be coupled with Christian responsibility, so as not to stumble our "weaker brethren" (1 Corinthians 8:7-13). The same principle applies to the giving and receiving of red thread and red packets.
19. Bong Rin Ro (ed.); op. cit.; pages 123-124.
20. Our dearly departed are believed to lead a life in the nether

world very similar to that of their past embodied state. McDougall notes the widespread custom of "burying or burning with the body of the dead man his most valued possessions, especially weapons and ornaments, due to the belief that even these things have their shadow duplicates or ghost-souls, which can be carried away by the departing soul and used by it as the real objects were used by the living man." William McDougall; op. cit.; page 2.

21. Bong Rin Ro (ed.); op. cit.; page 129.
22. D.A. MacKenzie; *China and Japan;* New York: Avenel Books; 1986; page 142f.
23. Bong Rin Ro; op. cit.; page 128-129.
24. Arthur Chern; *Anglicanism;* Singapore; 1992; page 59.
25. Jean-Jacques von Allmen; *Worship: Its Theology and Practice;* London: Lutterworth; 1965; page 269.
26. R.F. Patterson (ed.); *New Expanded Webster's Dictionary;* Miami, Florida: P.S.I. and Associates, Incorporated; 1989; pages 286 and 365.
27. For further reading, see David Burnett; *Clash of Worlds;* Eastbourne: Monarch Publications Limited; 1990.
28. S.B. Ferguson and D.F. Wright (eds.); op. cit.; page 230.
29. Though we may address the saints in heaven, nothing in the Bible advocates the efficacy of these saints to answer us, grant our requests or petition God on our behalf. This is not the idea behind the Doctrine of the Communion of Saints. An issue encountered is the use of the word "prayer", when referring to our fellowship with the saints in heaven. This usage should be avoided, due to its connotation of being a formula for worship, an address to God, and a solemn petition (to God).

30. "In time, it is taken to mean the fellowship of Christians in every age, past, present and future. In space, it means that all true believers are united in fellowship, regardless of nationality, language or culture." S.B. Ferguson and D.F. Wright (eds.); op. cit.; pages 152,153.
31. While celebrating Easter communion as a political prisoner in Paraguay, a pastor told those imprisoned with him of a man of about 60, whose daughter had died while fighting with the guerillas. The pastor shared that this man had said, "I think this communion means that our dead are alive, that they have given their bodies and blood, making Christ's sacrifice their own. I believe in the resurrection of the dead and feel their presence among us." Allowing for a moment of silence, the pastor continued with the Easter celebration and said, "This communion is not only a communion between us here but a communion with all our brothers and sisters in the church or outside. Not only those who are alive, but those too who have already died. Still more, it is a communion with those who will come after us and who will be faithful to Jesus Christ." Gwen K. Neville and John H. Westerhoff III; *Learning through Liturgy;* New York: The Seabury Press; 1978; page 131.
32. A parable is a story that is used to communicate a point.
33. E. John Hamlin; *A Guide to Isaiah 40-66;* TEF Study Guide 16; London: SPCK; 1979; page 180.

Traditional Chinese Medicine

1. Kao Chen; "Traditional Chinese Medicine: A Cure for All?"; *The Straits Times;* Singapore: Singapore Press Holdings

Limited; 19 August 2001.

2. Drawn from comments by Malaysian Minister Datuk Chua Jui Meng who was reported as saying that the Malaysian Health Ministry was drawing up a national policy that would incorporate traditional medicine into total health care. "Folk Medicine To Be Part Of Nation's Health-Care System"; *The Straits Times;* Singapore: Singapore Press Holdings Limited; 10 April 1996.

3. This image is taken from Paul C. Reisser, Teri K. Reisser, and John Weldon; *New Age Medicine;* Illinois: Inter-Varsity Press; 1987; page 57.

4. The following is an extract from the *Huai Nan Tzu* (circa 120 BC), a study of natural philosophy recorded in 21 volumes, with regard to the creation of *yin* and *yang*. "Before heaven and earth had taken form all was vague and amorphous. Therefore it was called the Great Beginning. The Great Beginning produced emptiness, and emptiness produced the universe. The universe produced material forces, which had limits. That which was clear and light drifted up to become heaven, while that which was heavy and turgid solidified to become earth. It was very easy for the pure, fine material to come together, but extremely difficult for the heavy turgid material to solidify. Therefore heaven was completed first and earth assumed shape afterwards. The combined essences of heaven and earth became *yin* and *yang*, the concentrated essences of *yin* and *yang* became the four seasons, and the scattered essences of the four seasons became the myriad creatures of the world. After a long time, the hot forces of the accumulated *yang* produced fire and the essence of the fire force became the

sun; the cold force of accumulated *yin* became water and the essence of the water became the moon. The essence of the excess force of the sun and moon became the stars and planets. Heaven received the sun, moon and stars, while earth received water and soil." Joanne O'Brien and Kwok Man Ho; *The Elements of Feng Shui;* Britain: Element Books Limited; 1991; pages 11 and 12.

5. "Asian Cures a Big Hit in the West"; *The Straits Times;* Singapore: Singapore Press Holdings Limited; 9 October 1996.
6. Allison Lim; "2 New Drug Finds for Cancer Patients"; *The Straits Times;* Singapore: Singapore Press Holdings Limited; 11 February 1997.
7. Indrani Nadarajah; "Chinese Herb Is New Anti-Malaria Drug Hope"; *The Straits Times;* Singapore: Singapore Press Holdings Limited; 5 August 1996.
8. Kao Chen; "Using Science to Make a Point about Acupuncture"; *The Straits Times;* Singapore: Singapore Press Holdings Limited; 19 August 2001.
9. The proponents of Traditional Chinese Medicine (TCM) "say that its 5,000 years of history represents the best clinical evidence that it works. But its critics maintain that TCM theory is not anatomically correct, and that its efficacy is based on anecdotal evidence and that its reliability is an issue." Kao Chen; "Traditional Chinese Medicine: A Cure for All?"; *The Straits Times;* Singapore: Singapore Press Holdings Limited; 19 August 2001.
10. "Provisional List of Treatable Diseases"; *The Straits Times;* Singapore: Singapore Press Holdings Limited; 23 March 1996.
11. Kao Chen; "Using Science to Make a Point about Acupuncture"; *The Straits Times;* Singapore: Singapore Press

Holdings Limited; 19 August 2001.

12. Compare *China's Qigong Therapy;* China: Shandong Science and Technology Press; 1985 and *Qigong: Essentials for Health Promotion;* China: China Reconstructs Press; 1988.
13. *Qigong: Essentials for Health Promotion;* China: China Reconstructs Press; 1988
14. M. Page; *The Power of Ch'i;* Aquarian Press; 1984.

Appendix A: *Long*, the Chinese Dragon

1. Mircea Eliade (editor-in-chief); *The Encyclopaedia of Religion, Volume 4*; New York: MacMillan Publishing Company; 1987; page 432.
2. Ong Hean-Tatt; *Chinese Animal Symbolism*; Malaysia: Pelanduk Publications (M) Sendirian Berhad; 1993; page 60.
3. The dragon was most probably chosen to represent Satan, due to the fear the image would naturally engender among the recipients of the Bible at the time, that is, the people of the ancient Middle Eastern world.
4. Mircea Eliade; op. cit.; page 432.
5. This could be due to the fact that snakes of the Middle Eastern world were both large and deadly. See Philip W. Goetz (editor-in-chief); *The New Encyclopaedia Britannica, Incorporated;* 15th Edition, 1991; page 209.
6. Ong Hean-Tatt; op. cit.; pages 61-63.
7. Some Charismatics and Pentecostals advocate that there are demonic spirits attached to idolatrous idols and images, which may either oppress or possess any who own or are in possession of the idols. A prime example of this belief is the attitude taken towards the Asian dragon, the image

of which in any form — be it a figurine, batik impression or design on a teapot or an urn — needs to be immediately destroyed to prevent demonic oppression or possession.

8. An article written by Kua Wee Seng for the Trinity Theological College magazine clearly shows this to be a hermeneutically (that is, interpretatively) wrong application of the Revelation text. Kua Wee Seng; "Interpreting the Dragon of Revelation 12"; *Trumpet Magazine;* Singapore: Trinity Theological College; 1992.
9. For example, the symbolic image of the lion is used in different places in the Bible to refer to both the Lion of Judah (Revelation 5:5) and the roaring lion (Satan) prowling around seeking for someone to devour (1 Peter 5:8).
10. The dragon is deemed to be predominantly good, albeit with a certain amount of evil — of its scales totalling 117, 81 are imbued with good influence (*yang*) and 36 with bad influence (*yin*). D. A. MacKenzie; *China And Japan; Myths and Legends Series*; New York: Avenel Books; 1986; page 46.
11. The high regard with which the dragon is held may best be seen in the dragon motif embroidered on the garments won by the emperors of ancient China, to signify both royalty and power. Evelyn Lip; *Chinese Temples and Deities;* Singapore: Times Books International; 1986, pages 12,13.
12. Chinese tradition holds that there are four *long wang* (dragon kings) ruling over the four seas, each with its own court ministers and army. *Longs* are also said to watch over all the waterways and have been assigned by the Jade Emperor of heaven to ensure regular rainfall over the land. The four major dragons of Chinese mythology are the celestial dragon (which protects the place of the gods), the spiritual

dragon (which controls wind and rain), the earth dragon (which controls the rivers and waters), and the underwater dragon (which guards precious metals and gems). Choo Bee Yian; "Enter the Dragons"; *The Straits Times;* Singapore: Singapore Press Holdings Limited; 1999.

13. It is noted that in Chinese philosophy, the *long* is the symbol of the Great Man; while in Chinese *feng shui*, the energy forces affecting human destiny are deemed to be "destiny lines". The Chinese also advocate that their emperor is *Long*, seated on "the *Long* (dragon) throne and wearing the *Long* robes of gold". Ong Hean-Tatt; op. cit.; page 56.
14. Simon Chan; "Christian Superstition"; *Impact Magazine,* Volume 16, Number 4; Singapore: Impact Christian Communications Limited; August-September 1992; pages 11-13.
15. E.T.C. Werner; *Myths and Legends of China;* London: George G. Harrap and Co.; 1958; pages 208-235.

Appendix B: An Attempt at Christianizing

1. In a study of the festivals of different religions, we note that many originated as harvest festivals, or as festivals celebrating the arrival of the spring rain. For example, originally, *Qing Ming Jie,* Easter and the Jewish Feast of Pentecost were all festivals celebrating the arrival of the spring rains. This celebration of thanksgiving for the advent of the spring rains is a fairly universally observed event. Over time, this celebration was separately incorporated into Judaism (the Feast of Pentecost), Christianity (Easter) and Chinese religious practice (*Qing Ming Jie*), and given their respective religious meanings and doctrinal basis.

Appendix C: The Scale of Veneration

1. Taken from the unpublished lectures on Asian Theology by Dr Simon Chan at Trinity Theological College in 1992.

Appendix E: Food Offered to Idols

1. Walter Bruggemann; *Genesis;* Interpretation; Atlanta, Georgia: John Knox Press; 1982; page 83.
2. George A. Buttrick (comm. ed.); *The Interpreter's Bible, Volume 1;* New York: Abingdon Press; 1952; page 550.
3. George A. Buttrick (comm. ed.); ibid.; page 550.
4. Peter C. Craigie; *The Book of Deuteronomy;* NICOT; Grand Rapids, Michigan: William B. Eerdmans Publishing Company; 1976; page 18.

Bibliography

Beaver, R. Pierce (con. ed., et. al.); *The World's Religions*; England: Lion's Publishing plc; First paperback edition, 1988

Benko, Stephen; *The Meaning Of Sanctorum Communio*; Neperville, Illinois: Alec R. Allenson Incoporated; 1964

Bevan, Edwyn; *Holy Images*; London: George Allen and Unwin Limited; 1940

Blofeld, John; *Taoism, The Quest For Immortality*; London: Unwin Limited; Reprinted, 1989.

Brown, Colin (gen. ed.); *The New International Dictionary Of New Testament Theology, Volume 1*; Regency Reference Library; Grand Rapids, Michigan: Zondervan Publishing House; 1986

Brown, David A.; *A Guide To Religions*; England: SPCK; 1987

Bruce, F.F.; *The Book Of Acts*; Grand Rapids, Michigan: William B. Eerdmans Publishing Company; Reprinted 1992

Brueggemann, Walter; *Genesis*; Interpretation; Atlanta, Georgia: John Knox Press; 1982

Burnett, David; *Unearthly Powers*; Eastbourne: Monarch Publications Limited; 1988

Burnett, David; *Clash Of Worlds*; Eastbourne: Monarch Publications Limited; 1990

Burnett, David; *The Spirit Of Hinduism*; Eastbourne: MARC; 1992

Buttrick, George Arthur; *The Interpreter's Bible, Volume 1*; Nashville, Tennessee: Abingdon Press; 1952

Chan, Simon; "Christian Superstition"; *Impact Magazine*, Volume 16, Number 4; Singapore: Impact Christian Communications Limited; August-September 1992

Chamberlain, Jonathan; *Chinese Gods*; Malaysia: Pelanduk Publications (Malaysia) Sendirian Berhad; 1987.

Chao, Samuel H.; *Confucian Chinese And The Gospel: Methodological Considerations; The Asia Journal of Theology Volume 1 Number 1, Yeow Choo Lak (ed.)*; Bangalore, India: North East Asia Association of Theological Schools; 1987.

Chern, Arthur S.C.; *Anglicanism*; Singapore; 1992

Choo Bee Yian; "Enter The Dragons"; *The Straits Times*; Singapore: Singapore Press Holdings Limited; 1999

Craigie, Peter C.; *The Book Of Deuteronomy*; Grand Rapids, Michigan: William B. Eerdmans Publishing Company; 1976

Eire, Carlos M.N.; *War Against The Idols*; Cambridge: Cambridge University Press; 1986

Eliade, Mircea (ed.-in-chief); *The Encyclopaedia Of Religion, Volumes 4 And 7*; New York: MacMillan Publishing Company; 1987

Enns, Paul; *The Moody Handbook Of Theology*; Chicago: Moody Press; 1989

Fee, Gordon; *The First Epistle To The Corinthians*; NICNT; Grand Rapids, Michigan: William B. Eerdmans Publishing Company; Reprinted 1988

Ferguson, Sinclair B. and Wright, David F. (eds.); *New Dictionary Of Theology*; Leicester, England: Inter-Varsity Press; Reprinted 1989

Foulkes, Francis; *Ephesians*; TNTC; Grand Rapids, Michigan: William B. Eerdmans Publishing Company; 1983

Goetz, Philip W. (ed.-in-chief); *The New Encyclopaedia Britannica, Volume 4*;

Chicago: Encyclopaedia Britannica, Incorporated; 15th edition, 1991

Granet, Marcel; *The Religion Of The Chinese People*; New York: Harper and Row; 1975

Grant, R.M.; *Gods And The One God*; Philadelphia, USA: Westminster Press; 1986

Guthrie, Donald; *New Testament Theology*; Leicester, England: Inter-Varsity Press; Reprinted 1985

Hamlin, E. John; *A Guide To Isaiah 40-66*; TEF Study Guide 16; London: SPCK; 1979

Hughes, P.E.; *The Second Epistle To The Corinthians*; NICNT; Grand Rapids, Michigan: William B. Eerdmans Publishing Company; 1988

Jochim, Christian; *Chinese Religions*; Englewood Cliffs, New Jersey: Prentice Hall Incorporated; 1986

Kao Chen; "Using Science To Make A Point About Acupuncture"; *The Straits Times*; Singapore: Singapore Press Holdings Limited; 19 August 2001

Kua Wee Seng; "Interpreting The Dragon Of Revelation 12"; *Trumpet Magazine*; Singapore: Trinity Theological College; 1992

Lee-Wang Cheng Yang; *Chasing The Dragon: A Bibliographic Pursuit*; Trinity Theological College Journal, Volume 6; Singapore: Trinity Theological College; 1996

Leong Heng Keng (chairman, Committee on Chinese Customs and Rites); *Chinese Customs And Festivals In Singapore*; Singapore: Singapore Federation of Chinese Clan Associations; 1989

Lim, Allison; "2 New Drug Finds For Cancer Patients"; *The Straits Times*; Singapore: Singapore Press Holdings Limited; 11 February 1997

Lip, Evelyn; *Chinese Temples And Deities*; Singapore: Times Books International; 1986

Lip, Evelyn; *Chinese Beliefs And Superstitions*; Singapore: Graham Brash Private Limited; 1988

MacKenzie, Donald A.; *China And Japan*; Myths And Legends Series; New York: Avenel Books; 1986

McCauliffe, C.S.J.; *Sacramental Theology*; London: B. Herder Book Company; Revised edition 1961

McDougall, William; *Body And Mind*; London: Methuen Publishers; Eighth edition, 1938

McDowell, Josh; *Understanding Non-Christian Religions*; California, USA: Here's Life Publishers; 1982

Modder, R.P.; *Chinese Temple Festivals: Origins Of Religious Beliefs*; Hong Kong: South China Morning Post; 1983

Nadarajah, Indrani; "Chinese Herb Is New Anti-Malaria Drug Hope"; *The Straits Times*; Singapore: Singapore Press Holdings Limited; 5 August 1996

Neville, Gwen K. and Westerhoss III, John H.; *Learning Through Liturgy*; New York: The Seabury Press; 1978

North, Gary; *Unholy Spirits: Occultism And New Age Humanism*; USA: Dominion Press; 1988

O'Brien, Joanne and Kwok Man Ho; *The Elements Of Feng Shui*; Britain: Element Books Limited; 1991

Ong Hean-Tatt; *Chinese Animal Symbolisms*; Malaysia: Pelanduk Publications (M) Sendirian Berhad; 1993

Page, M.; *The Power Of Ch'i*; Aquarian Press; 1984

Patterson, R.F. (ed.); *New Expanded Webster's Dictionary*; Miami, Florida: P.S.I. Associates, Incorporated; 1989 edition

Reichelt, K.L.; *Religion In Chinese Garment*; London: Lutterworth Press; 1951

Reisser, Paul C., Reisser, Teri K. and Weldon, John; *New Age Medicine*; Illinois: Inter-Varsity Press; 1987

Ridenour, Fritz; *So What's The Difference*; Ventura, USA: Regal Books; 1967

Ro, Bong Rin (ed.); *Christian Alternatives To Ancestor Practices*; Taiwan:

Asian Theological Association; 1985

Royal Anthropological Institute; *Notes And Queries On Anthropology*; London: Routledge and Kegan Paul; 1951

Schoenbart, Bill; *Chinese Healing Secrets: Time-Tested Ways To Help Your Body Heal Itself*; Illinois: Publications International, Limited; 1997

Smith, Henry N.; "Ancestor Practices In Contemporary Hong Kong: Religious Ritual Or Social Custom?"; *The Asia Journal of Theology*, Volume 3, Number 1; Bangalore, India: North East Asia Association of Theological Schools; 1989.

Sng, Bobby and Choong Chee Pang (eds.); *Church And Culture*; Singapore: Graduates Christian Fellowship; February 1991

Sunquist, Scott W. (ed.); *A Dictionary of Asian Christianity*; Grand Rapids, Michigan: William B. Eerdmans Publishing Company; 2001

Tan, Lucy; *The Christian Answer To Ancestral Worship*; Selangor, Malaysia: Asian Beacon Fellowship; Fourth print, 1981

Thera, Narada; *Parents And Children*; Singapore: Singapore Buddhist Mission; 1990.

Tillich, Paul; *Dynamics Of Faith*; New York: Harper and Brothers Publishers; 1957

Von Allmen, Jean-Jacques; *Worship, Its Theology And Practice*; London: Lutterworth; 1965

Wagner, C. Peter; *Warfare Prayer*; Ventura, California: Regal Books; 1992

Warneck, Johannes G.; *The Living Forces Of The Gospel*; Edinburgh: Oliphant, Anderson and Ferrier; 1909

Wenham, Gordon J.; *The Book Leviticus*; NICOT; Grand Rapids, Michigan: William B. Eerdmans Publishing Company; 1979

Werner, E.T.C.; *Myths And Legends Of China*; London: George G. Harrap and Company; 1958

Wink, Walter; *Unmasking The Powers*; Philadelphia: Fortress Press; 1986

Wolf, Arthur P.; *Religion And Ritual In Chinese Society*; Stanford, California: Standford University Press; 1974

Wong Fong Yang; *Freedom And Consideration: The Christian's Dilemma Concerning Food Offered To Idols*; Selangor, Malaysia: Pustaka SUFES Sendirian Berhad; 1994

"Asian Cures A Big Hit In The West", *The Straits Times*; Singapore: Singapore Press Holdings Limited; 9 October 1996

China's Qigong Therapy; China: Shandong Science And Technology Press; 1985

"Folk Medicine To Be Part Of Nation's Health-Care System"; *The Straits Times*; Singapore: Singapore Press Holdings Limited; 10 April 1996

"Provisional List of Treatable Diseases"; *The Straits Times*; Singapore: Singapore Press Holdings Limited; 23 March 1996

Qigong: Essentials For Health Promotion; China: China Reconstructs Press; 1988

OTHER TITLES FROM ARMOUR PUBLISHING

A CHRISTIAN PERSPECTIVE ON HEALTH AND WELLNESS

In this book, Alan Ch'ng frames health and wellness strategies for readers that focus on areas such as exercise, nutrition, weight control, stress and self-esteem. He also shares how Christians can achieve spiritual fitness by living a God-centred life. In the end, if health fails, the believer who puts his hope in God can still hold his head high and praise his Creator.

ISBN 981-4045-45-4

**A CHRISTIAN RESPONSE
TO THE LIFE SCIENCES**

This book provides both a basic background to the life sciences, as well as Christian ethical foundations. Other chapters then build on these to deal with cloning, embryonic stem cell research, the human genome project and genetically modified food. The result of team work, these issues are covered both from the scientific view — what is, what is involved — and the Christian view, how Christian biblical and theological principles guide our understanding of and response to these issues.

ISBN 981-4045-31-4

A LIVING SACRIFICE

We often interpret Paul's exhortation in the Bible that we should offer up our bodies as a living sacrifice to mean that we need to give of our time and energies in God's service. Anthony Yeo points out, in his inimitably forthright way, that our physical bodies are also part and parcel of this act of spiritual worship.

ISBN 981-4045-20-9

PARTNERS IN LIFE

Written specifically in the context of Singapore and its neighbouring regions, this book provides eye-opening, myth-shattering information and counsel, as well as refreshing, common-sensical perspectives to marital situations.

ISBN 981-4045-31-4